FRESH DESIGNS
MITTENS AND GLOVES

FEATURING DESIGNS BY

Anna Dalvi
Ellen Boucher
Laura Nelkin
Laura Patterson
Rebecca Blair
Ruth Garcia-Alcantud
Sara Peterson
Sarah Eyre
Sarah Wilson
Sharon Fuller

AND PHOTOGRAPHY BY

Robert Gladys / Fractured Photography

COOPERATIVE PRESS
Cleveland, OH
cooperativepress.com

FRESH DESIGNS: MITTENS AND GLOVES

Library of Congress Control Number: 2012953296
ISBN 13: 978-1-937513-2c-7
First Edition
Published by Cooperative Press
http://www.cooperativepress.com

Patterns © 2013, their designers, as credited
Photos © 2013, Robert Gladys, Fractured Photography (fracturedphotography.com), unless otherwise noted

Makeup by Elle Gemma, Spell Cosmetics (spellcosmetics.com)
Models: Arabella Proffer, Elle Gemma, Rachel Harner, Susan Prahst, Terra Incognita

Every effort has been made to ensure that all the information in this book is accurate at the time of publication; however, Cooperative Press neither endorses nor guarantees the content of external links referenced in this book.

If you have questions or comments about this book, or need information about licensing, custom editions, special sales, or academic/corporate purchases, please contact Cooperative Press: info@cooperativepress.com or 13000 Athens Ave C288, Lakewood, OH 44107 USA

No part of this book may be reproduced in any form, except brief excerpts for the purpose of review, without prior written permission of the publisher. Thank you for respecting our copyright.

FOR COOPERATIVE PRESS

Senior Editor: Shannon Okey
Assistant Editor: Elizabeth Green Musselman
Developmental Editor: Atra Forman
Technical Editor: Alexand`a Virgiel
Cover Designer: Tamas Jakab
Production Manager: MJ Kim

TABLE OF CONTENTS

ANNA DALVI	Norse Mitts	(page 5)
ELLEN BOUCHER	Bella	(page 11)
LAURA NELKIN	Mock Cable Techno Mittens	(page 15)
LAURA PATTERSON	Acantha	(page 19)
REBECCA BLAIR	Bangles	(page 23)
RUTH GARCIA-ALCANTUD	Kelly	(page 27)
SARA PETERSON	Equus Quagga	(page 31)
SARAH EYRE	Asylum Hill	(page 37)
SARAH WILSON	Cabletilt	(page 41)
SHARON FULLER	Empyrean	(page 47)
ACKNOWLEDGMENTS		(page 53)
ABBREVIATIONS		(page 54)
ABOUT COOPERATIVE PRESS & THE FRESH DESIGNS SERIES		(page 55)

NORSE MITTS

BY ANNA DALVI

These mittens are warmer than most, because the double-knitting creates two layers of fabric. They are fully reversible and feature Norse motifs around the cuff and on the hand.

DIFFICULTY
EXPERIENCED

SIZES
M [L] (shown in size M)

FINISHED MEASUREMENTS
Hand circumference: 7 [7.75]"/18 [19.5]cm
Length: 10.75 [11.75]"/27.5 [30]cm

MATERIALS
Lisa Souza Sock! Merino [100% merino wool; 560yds/512m per 113g skein]
- [MC] St. Valentine (red); 1 skein
- [CC] Ice Ice Baby (white); 1 skein

1 32-inch US #0/2mm circular needle or set of dpns, as preferred, for size M
1 32-inch US #1/2.25mm circular needle or set of dpns, as preferred, for size L
1 32-inch US #2.5/3.0mm circular needle or 2 dpns, for both sizes
Cable needle
Yarn needle
Stitch marker
Waste yarn

GAUGE
29 sts/42 rows = 4"/10cm in double-knit St st on US #0/2mm needle for size M
26 sts/38 rows = 4"/10cm in double-knit St st on US #1/2.25mm needle for size L

PATTERN NOTES
Double knitting is knitting with two colors in such a way that the knitted fabric is reversible, and the colors of the pattern are inverted. The two sides look like stockinette knitting, and the fabric is double-thick for extra warmth.

For double knitting, each square in the chart represents TWO stitches. You knit the stitch with the pattern color that should face you, and then you purl the next stitch with the other color.

For each stitch, take both strands to the back when knitting and both to the front when purling. Ensure that the strands are never twisted.

Pattern assumes you are working in the round using the "magic loop" method on a long circular needle, but dpns or two circulars can be used instead.

PATTERN
MITTEN (BOTH ALIKE)
Hand:
With US #2.5/3mm needle(s), CO 4 sts. Make I-cord as foll: Knit 1 row. *Do not turn work, but slide sts back to working end of needle, draw yarn firmly across back of work, and knit the row again. Rep from * for a total of 50 rows. Break yarn but do not bind off. Place sts on a piece of waste yarn.

Using smaller needle(s), beg at cast-on end, pick up sts from the I-cord as foll: *Pick up and knit 1 st with MC, pick up and purl 1 st with CC; rep from * in each row of the I-cord, for a total of 100 sts (50 in each color). Pm and join in the round, being careful not to twist. Begin working Chart A.

After a few rnds of Chart A have been worked, graft the end of the I-cord to the beginning, and weave in ends.

Work to end of Chart A, then work Chart B through Rnd 27. On Rnd 27, after working the 38 sts bordered in blue (19 knit sts and 19 purl sts), place them on waste yarn for the thumb. Work Chart C with rem sts.

After completing Chart C, 8 sts remain (4 knit sts and 4 purl sts). Separate the stitches for inside and outside of the mitten. Break CC, and use a yarn needle to thread the tail through all the sts on the inside of the mitten (all purl sts), twice. Pull tight. Break MC, and thread through all the sts or the outside of the mitten (all knit sts), twice. Pull tight. Weave in both ends between the layers so they are invisible.

Thumb:
Place the 38 held sts back on the needles and work Chart D. The first pair of sts on the chart necs to be picked up from the yo on Rnd 1 of Chart C—k1 MC, p1 CC into that st.
The second pair of sts is picked up in the gap between the yo on Rnd 1 of Chart C and the first sts now on the needles.
The last pair of sts on the chart is picked up in the gap between the sts on the needles and the yo on Rnd 1 of Chart C. The thumb is then worked in the round.
After completing Chart D, 20 sts remain on the thumb (10 knit sts and 10 purl sts). Separate the stitches for inside and outside of the mitten. Break CC, and use a yarn needle to thread tail through all the stitches on the inside of the mitten, twice. Pull tight. Break MC, and thread through all the stitches on the outside of the mitten, twice. Pull tight. Weave in both ends between the layers so they are invisible.

FINISHING
Block as desired.

ABOUT THE DESIGNER
Anna is originally from the west coast of Sweden, but has traded the rugged cliffs of Bohuslän for the Canadian wilderness. In her knitting, Anna enjoys variety more than anything else—from intricate lace to sprawling cables, and differences in color and texture. Her designs can be found at www.knitandknag.com or on Ravelry, where she goes by knitandknag.

CHART A

LEGEND FOR ALL NORSE MITTS CHARTS

- ☐ k1 with CC, p1 with MC
- 🟧 k1 with MC, p1 with CC
- k1tbl with MC, p1tbl with CC
- k1tbl with CC, p1tbl with MC
- yo with MC, yo with CC
- yo with CC, yo with MC
- pick up 1 st and knit with CC, pick up 1 st and purl with MC
- pick up 1 st and knit with MC, pick up 1 st and purl with CC
- left dec MC facing: sl1 kwise, sl1 onto cn and hold behind work, sl1 kwise, replace 2 sts from right ndl on left ndl and k2tog tbl with MC, replace st from cn on left ndl and p2tog with CC
- left dec CC facing: sl1 kwise, sl1 onto cn and hold behind work, sl1 kwise, replace 2 sts from right ndl on left ndl and k2tog tbl with CC, replace st from cn on left ndl and p2tog with MC
- right dec MC facing: sl1 pwise, sl1 kwise onto cn and hold behind work, replace st from right ndl on left ndl and k2tog with MC, sl1 kwise onto cn, p2tog tbl from cn with CC
- right dec CC facing: sl1 pwise, sl1 kwise onto cn and hold behind work, replace st from right ndl on left ndl and k2tog with CC, sl1 kwise onto cn, p2tog tbl from cn with MC
- ⬛ no stitch

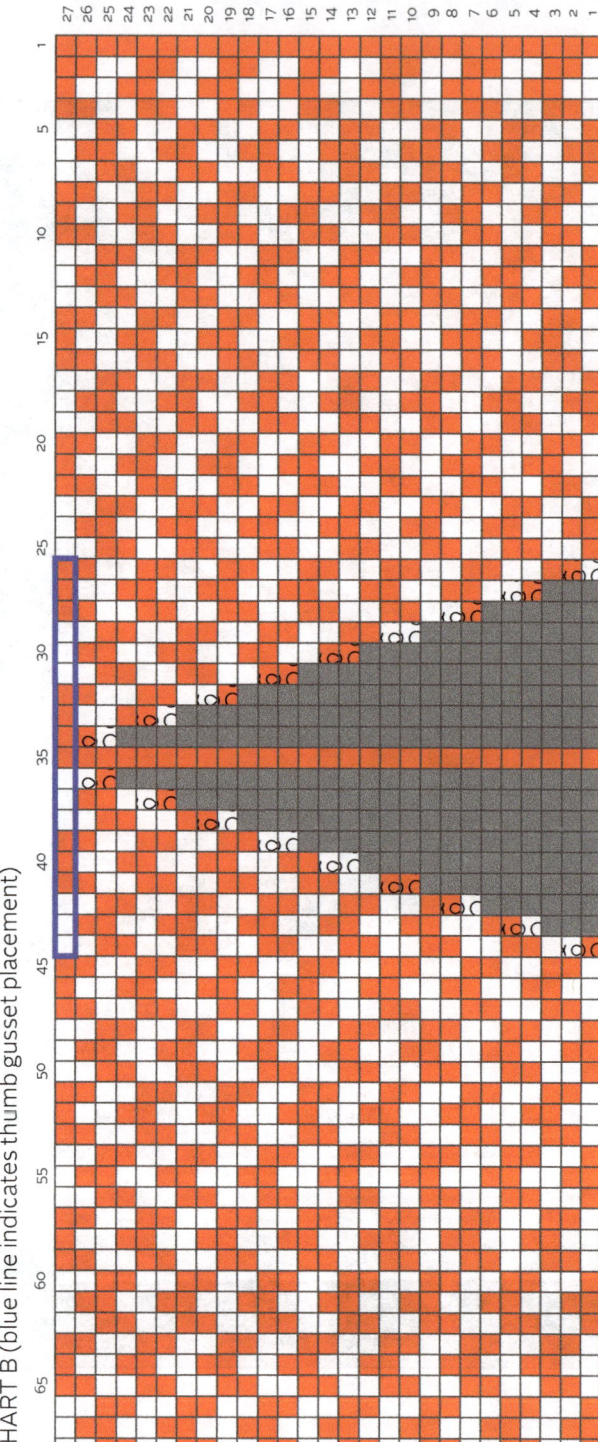

CHART B (blue line indicates thumb gusset placement)

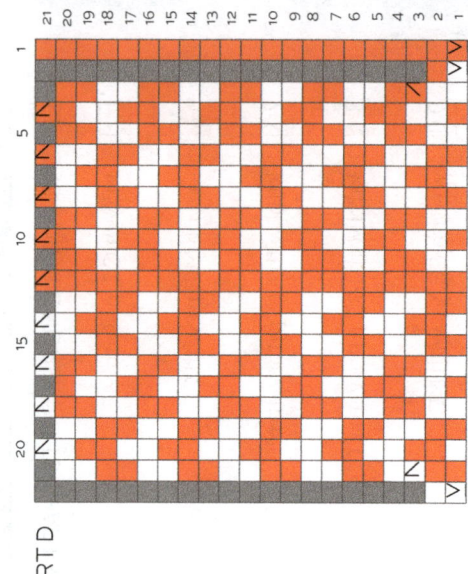

CHART D

CHART C

BELLA

BY ELLEN BOUCHER

Bella is dedicated to Jenni and Anna, and the bell ringers of St. Michael's Church. The cables follow a bell ringing method called Grandsire Doubles. The gloves can be warm yet classically glamorous evening wear, or if made fingerless could keep you toasty but stylish in an air-conditioned office.

DIFFICULTY
EXPERIENCED

SIZES
S [M, L] (shown in size M)

FINISHED MEASUREMENTS
Hand circumference: 7.25 [8, 8.75]"/18.5 [20.5, 22]cm

MATERIALS
Needle Food Merino Worsted [100% wool; 267yds/244m per 150g skein]; color: Blue Teal; 2 skeins

Set of US #7/4.5mm dpns
Cable needle
Waste yarn
Stitch markers

GAUGE
19 sts/26 rows = 4"/10cm in St st

PATTERN

LEFT GLOVE

Arm:
CO 46 [50, 54] sts, divide evenly over needles, pm and join to work in the round. Work in p1, k1 rib for 9 rnds.
Pattern set up rnd: Work Rnd 1 of Cable Chart over 31 sts, pm, k15 [19, 23].
Next rnd: Work next rnd of Cable Chart, sm, knit to end.
Continue as set by last rnd through Rnd 12 of Chart.
Dec rnd: Work next rnd of Cable Chart, sm, k2tog, knit to last 2 sts, ssk. 44 [48, 52] sts rem.

Work even in established patts through end of Chart. 38 [42, 46] sts rem. Piece measures approx. 13.25"/33.5cm from cast on.
Work in p1, k1 rib for 7 rnds.

Hand:
Inc rnd: Knit, inc 8 [10, 10] sts evenly spaced. 46 [52, 56] sts.
Work even in St st until hand measures 3.25 [3.25, 3.5]"/8.5 [8.5, 9]cm from top of ribbing.

Set up for thumb: Knit to last 7 [8, 8] sts. Place the next 14 [16, 16] sts on waste yarn. Use the backward loop method to CO 1 st, knit to end of rnd. 34 [38, 42] sts.

Work even in St st until hand measures 3 [3.25, 3.5]"/7.5 [8.5, 9]cm from top of ribbing.

Index finger:
With back of hand facing, k6 [6, 7], place next 22 [25, 28] sts on waste yarn, use backward loop method to CO 3 sts, knit last 6 [7, 7] sts. 15 [16, 17] sts on needles. Work in the round until finger measures 3 [3, 3.25]"/7.5 [7.5, 8.5]cm from base. Next rnd: K1 [0, 1], [k2tog] 7 [8, 8] times. 8 [8, 9] sts. Cut yarn, thread through rem sts, pull tight and fasten off.

Middle finger:
With back of hand facing, slip next 5 [5, 6] sts from waste yarn to a needle. Turn work so palm is facing and slip 4 [5, 5] sts from other end of waste yarn to a second needle. Join yarn, k4 [5, 5], pick up and knit 3 sts from base of index finger, k5 [5, 6], CO 3 sts. 15 [16, 17] sts. Work in the round until finger measures 3.25 [3.25, 3.5]"/8.5 [8.5, 9]cm from base. Next rnd: K1 [0, 1], [k2tog] 7 [8, 8] times. 8 [8, 9] sts. Cut yarn, thread through rem sts, pull tight and fasten off.

Ring finger:
With back of hand facing, slip next 4 [5, 5] sts from waste yarn to a needle. Turn work so palm is facing and slip 4 [5, 5] sts from other end of waste yarn to a second needle. Join yarn, k4 [5, 5], pick up and knit 3 sts from base of middle finger, k4 [5, 5], CO 4 sts. 15 [16, 17] sts. Work in the round until finger measures 3 [3, 3.25]"/7.5 [7.5, 8.5]cm from base. Next rnd: K1 [0, 1], [k2tog] 7 [7, 8] times. 8 [8, 9] sts. Cut yarn, thread through rem sts, pull tight and fasten off.

Little finger:
Place rem 5 [6, 7] sts from waste yarn on needles. Join yarn, pick up and knit 4 sts from base of ring finger, knit to end. 9 [10, 11] sts. Work in the round until finger measures 2.25 [2.25, 2.5]"/5.5 [5.5, 6.5]cm from base. Next rnd: K1 [c, 1], [k2tog] 4 [5, 5] times. 5 [5, 6] sts. Cut yarn, thread through rem sts, pull tight and fasten off.

Thumb:
Place 14 [16, 16] sts from waste yarn on needles. Join yarn, pick up and knit 2 sts from cast on at crotch of hand, knit to end. 16 [18, 18] sts. Work in the round until thumb measures 2.5 [2.5, 2.75]"/6.5 [6.5, 7]cm from base. Next rnd: [k2tog] 8 [9, 9] times. 8 [9, 9] sts. Cut yarn, thread through rem sts, pull tight and fasten off.

RIGHT GLOVE

Arm:
Work same as for left glove.

Hand:
Inc rnd: Knit, inc 8 [10, 10] sts evenly spaced. 46 [52, 56] sts. Work even in St st until hand measures 3.25 [3.25, 3.5]"/8.5 [8.5, 9]cm from top of ribbing.

Set up for thumb: K16 [18, 20], place the next 14 [16, 16] sts on waste yarn. Use the backward loop method to CO 1 st, pm for new beg of rnd, CO 1 st, knit to end of rnd. 34 [38, 42] sts.

Work even in St st until hand measures 3 [3.25, 3.5]"/7.5 [8.5, 9]cm from top of ribbing.

Index finger:
With palm of hand facing, k6 [7, 7], place next 22 [25, 28] sts on waste yarn, use backward loop method to CO 3 sts, knit last 6 [6, 7] sts. 15 [16, 17] sts on needles. Work in the round until finger measures 3 [3, 3.25]"/7.5 [7.5, 8.5]cm from base. Next rnd: K1 [0, 1], [k2tog] 7 [8, 8] times. 8 [8, 9] sts. Cut yarn, thread through rem sts, pull tight and fasten off.

Middle finger:
With palm of hand facing, slip next 4 [5, 5] sts from waste yarn to a needle. Turn work so back of hand is facing and slip 5 [5, 6] sts from other end of waste yarn to a second needle. Join yarn, k5 [5, 6], pick up and knit 3 sts from base of index finger, k4 [5, 5], CO 3 sts. 15 [16, 17] sts. Work in the round until finger measures 3.25 [3.25, 3.5]"/8.5 [8.5, 9]cm from base. Next rnd: K1 [0, 1], [k2tog] 7 [8, 8] times. 8 [8, 9] sts. Cut yarn, thread through rem sts, pull tight and fasten off.

Ring finger:
With palm of hand facing, slip next 4 [4, 5] sts from waste yarn to a needle. Turn work so back of hand is facing and slip 4 [5, 5] sts from other end of waste yarn to a second needle. Join yarn, k4 [5, 5], pick up and knit 3 sts from base of middle finger, k4 [4, 5], CO 4 sts. 15 [16, 17] sts. Work in the round until finger measures 3 [3, 3.25]"/7.5 [7.5, 8.5]cm from base. Next rnd: K1 [0, 1], [k2tog] 7 [7, 8] times. 8 [8, 9] sts. Cut yarn, thread through rem sts, pull tight and fasten off.

Little finger:
Work same as for left glove.

Thumb:
Work same as for left glove.

FINISHING
Weave in ends. Wet block.

ABOUT THE DESIGNER
Ellen inherited her knitting prowess from her Nan, Dorothy, and her Great Aunt Enid, who taught her as a girl. She lives, crafts and plays pretend in Wellington, New Zealand, with an awesome costume wardrobe and a perfectly reasonable, nay austere, amount of yarn.

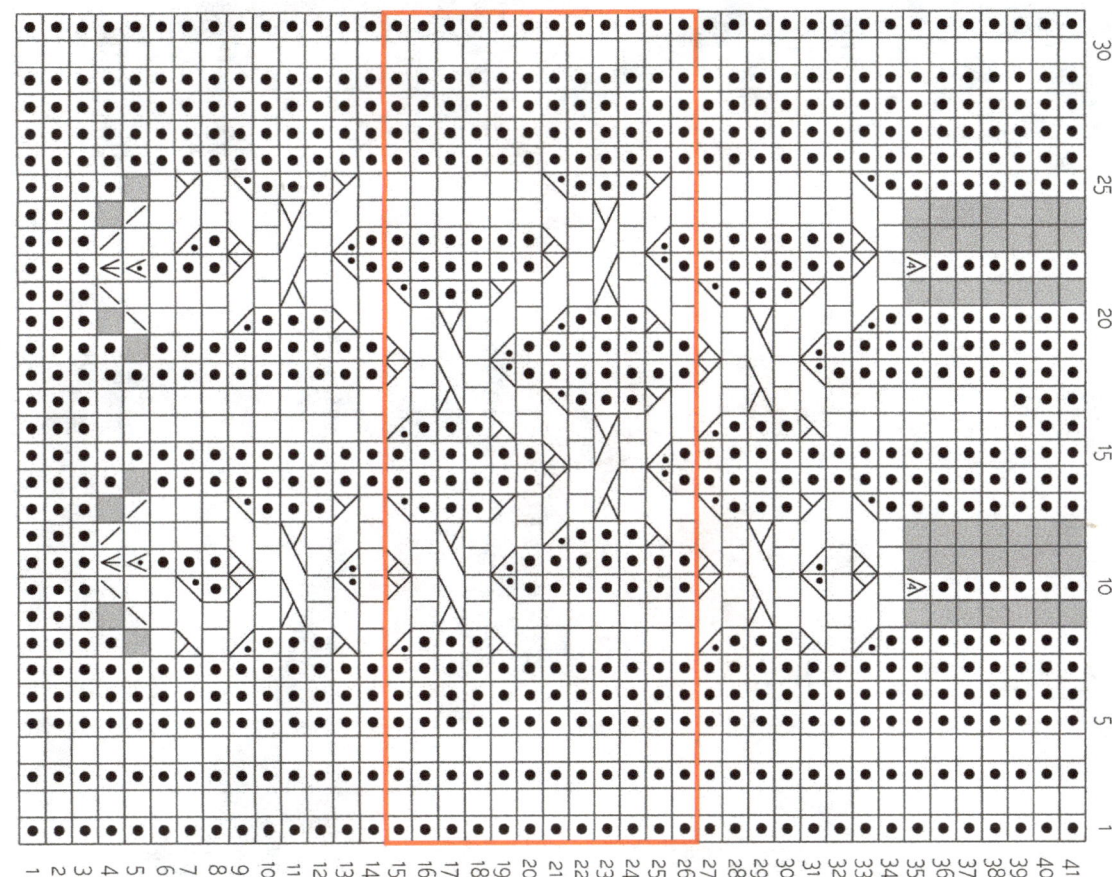

MOCK CABLE TECHNO MITTENS

BY LAURA NELKIN

DIFFICULTY
INTERMEDIATE

You are waiting for the bus, you are chilly and wearing your mittens, suddenly you get a text! What to do? Take off your mitten and answer it? No! All you have to do with these pretties is peel back the top of the thumb and flip back the top and you have all the digits necessary to take care of business and not freeze at the same time! Perfect, right? Knit at a tighter gauge on worsted weight yarn, with a dense mock cable this fabric is warm, wind proof, and pretty!

SIZES
Child 4-8 years [Adult XS, S, M, L] (Shown in size Adult XS)

FINISHED MEASUREMENTS
Hand circumference: 6.25 [7.75, 8.5, 9]"/16 [18, 19.5, 21.5, 23]cm
Length: 7.5 [9.25, 11, 12, 12.75]"/19 [23.5, 28, 30.5, 32.5]cm

MATERIALS
Schaefer Yarn Chris [80% extrafine superwash merino wool, 20% nylon; 215yds/196m per 113g skein]; color: Saffron; 1 [1, 2, 2, 2] skeins

Set of five US #4/3.5mm dpns
Stitch markers
Waste yarn
Yarn needle

GAUGE
22 sts/32 rnds = 4"/10cm in St st
37 sts/40 rnds = 4"/10cm in 2x1 Mock Cable Rib, unstretched

STITCHES
LT (left twist): Knit second st on left needle tbl and leave st on needle, knit first st on left needle tbl, slip both sts off needle.

2x2 Mock Cable Rib (multiple of 4 sts)
Rnds 1 and 2: *K1 tbl, k1 tbl, p2; rep from * to end.
Rnd 3: *LT, p2; rep from * to end.
Rep Rnds 1-3.

2x1 Mock Cable Rib (multiple of 3 sts)
Rnd 1: *K1 tbl, k1 tbl, p1; rep from * to end.
Rnd 2: *LT, p1; rep from * to end.
Rnd 3: Rep Rnd 1.
Rep Rnds 1-3.

PATTERN NOTES
The thumb hole is made just like a traditional buttonhole. You can skip it if your thumb doesn't need to see the light of day!

PATTERN
RIGHT MITTEN
Cuff
CO 36 [40, 44, 48, 52] sts, pm and join to work in the rnd. Work 2x2 Mock Cable Rib for 2.5 [3.5, 4, 4.5, 4.5]"/6.5 [9, 10, 11.5, 11.5] cm, ending with Rnd 3.
Hand set-up rnd: *K1 tbl, k1 tbl, (pfb) twice; rep from * 4 [4, 5, 5, 6] more times, knit to last st, kfb. 47 [51, 57, 61, 67] sts.

Thumb Gusset
Rnd 1: Work 2x1 Mock Cable Rib over 30 [30, 36, 36, 42] sts (back of hand), pm, m1L, p1, m1R, pm, knit to end. 2 sts inc'd.
Rnd 2: Work in patt to marker, sm, p3, sm, knit to end.
Rnd 3: Work in patt to marker, sm, m1L, purl to next marker, m1R, sm, knit to end. 2 sts inc'd.
Rnds 4 and 5: Work in patt to marker, sm, purl to next marker, sm, knit to end.
Rep Rnds 3-5 11 [13, 15, 17, 19] more times. 11 [13, 15, 17, 19] sts between the markers.

Sizes Child 4-8 yrs [Adult XS, S] only:
Next rnd: Work in patt to marker, remove marker, place next 11 [13, 15, 17, 19] sts on waste yarn for thumb, remove marker, CO 1 st, knit to end of rnd. 47 [51, 57, 61, 67] sts.

All sizes:
Work 1 rnd even.

15

Hand

Work 3 [3, 4, 5] rnds even, maintaining 2x1 Mock Cable Rib on back of hand and St st over palm.

Next rnd: Work to last 2 [3, 3, 3] sts, pm for new beg of rnd. Make a note of the last patt rnd worked.

Flap set-up rnd 1: (Kfb) 34 [36, 42, 42, 48] times (removing old marker when you come to it), knit to end.

Flap set-up rnd 2: (Place next st on waste yarn, k1) 34 [36, 42, 48] times, knit to end. The 34 [36, 42, 42, 48] sts on waste yarn will be used to knit the flap later. Make sure the held sts/waste yarn are on the outside of the mitten. 47 [51, 57, 61, 67] sts rem on needles.

Work 6 [8, 9, 11, 12] rnds even, maintaining 2x1 Mock Cable Rib over 30 [30, 36, 36, 42] sts on back of hand and St st over palm.

Edging

Rnd 1: (K2tog, p1) 11 [11, 13, 13, 15] times, *k1 tbl, p1; rep from * to end. 36 [40, 44, 48, 52] sts.

Rnd 2: *K1 tbl, p1; rep from * to end.

Rep last rnd 2 [2, 3, 3, 4] more times.

BO all sts in patt.

Flap

CO 17 [21, 21, 27, 27] sts onto one dpn. Place 34 [36, 42, 42, 48] flap sts from waste yarn on another 2 or 3 dpns. Work across all sts in next rnd of 2x1 Mock Cable Rib patt. Pm and join to work in the round. 51 [57, 63, 69, 75] sts. Work even in patt until mitten and flap together measure 6.5 [8, 9.5, 10.5, 11]"/16.5 [20.5, 24, 26.5, 28]cm from CO. Redistribute sts over needles as foll:

Needle 1: 15 [15, 18, 18, 21] sts
Needle 2: 12 [15, 15, 18, 18] sts
Needle 3: 12 [15, 15, 18, 18] sts
Needle 4: 12 [12, 15, 15, 18] sts

Shape top:

Dec rnd 1: (Work to last 2 sts on needle, p2tog) 4 times. 4 sts dec'd.

Rep Dec Rnd 1 on every rnd 10 [10, 13, 13, 16] more times. 7 [13, 7, 13, 7] sts rem.

Sizes - [Adult XS, -, M, -] only:
Dec rnd 2: (Work to last 2 sts on needle, p2tog) 3 times, p1. 3 sts dec'd.

Rep Dec Rnd 2 once more. - [7, -, 7, -] sts rem.

All sizes:
Cut yarn leaving a 6"/15cm tail, thread tail through rem 7 sts, and pull tight. Fasten off.

Thumb

Place 11 [13, 15, 17, 19] held thumb sts on needles, join yarn leaving a 6"/15cm tail and pick up 1 st from base of thumb, purl to end. 12 [14, 16, 18, 20] sts. Work even in reverse St st (purl every rnd) until thumb measures 1.25 [1.5, 1.75, 2, 2]"/3 [4, 4.5, 5, 5]cm, or reaches to the middle of the thumbnail.

Thumb Hole (optional):

Rnd 1: P8 [10, 12, 14, 15], BO 4 [4, 4, 4, 5] sts.

Rnd 2: P8 [10, 12, 14, 15], use backward loop method to CO 4 [4, 4, 4, 5] sts.

If you omit the thumb hole, work 2 rnds even here.

Decrease for top:

Rnd 1: (P2tog, p2 [2, 3, 4, 5]) twice, p2tog, p2 [4, 4, 4, 4]. 9 [11, 13, 15, 17] sts rem.

Rnd 2: Purl.

Rnd 3: (P2tog, p1 [1, 2, 3, 4]) twice, p2tog, p1 [3, 3, 3, 3]. 6 [8, 10, 12, 14] sts rem.

Rnd 4: Purl.

Rnd 5: (P2tog, po [0, 1, 2, 2]) twice, p2tog, po [2, 2, 2, 2]. 3 [5, 7, 9, 11] sts rem.

Sizes - [-, Adult S, M, L] only:
Rnd 6: Purl.
Rnd 7: (P2tog) - [-, 3, 4, 5] times, p1. - [-, 4, 5, 6] sts rem.

All sizes:
Cut yarn, thread tail through rem sts, and pull tight. Fasten off.

LEFT MITTEN

Cuff

CO 36 [40, 44, 48, 52] sts, pm and join to work in the rnd. Work 2x2 Mock Cable Rib for 2.5 [3.5, 4, 4.5, 4.5]"/6.5 [9, 10, 11.5, 11.5] cm, ending with Rnd 3.

Hand set-up rnd: Kfb, k15 [19, 19, 23, 23], *k1 tbl, k1 tbl, (pfb) twice; rep from * 4 [4, 5, 5, 6] more times. 47 [51, 57, 61, 67] sts.

Thumb Gusset

Rnd 1: K16 [20, 20, 24, 24], pm, m1L, p1, m1R, pm, work 2x1 Mock Cable Rib over 30 [30, 36, 36, 42] sts (back of hand). 2 sts inc'd.

Rnd 2: Knit to marker, sm, p3, sm, work in patt to end.

Rnd 3: Knit to marker, sm, m1L, purl to next marker, m1R, sm, work in patt to end. 2 sts inc'd.

Rnds 4 and 5: Knit to marker, sm, purl to next marker, sm, work in patt to end.

Rep Rnds 3-5 [4, 5, 6, 7] more times. 11 [13, 15, 17, 19] sts between the markers.

16

Sizes Child 4-8 yrs [Adult XS, S] only:
Work 1 rnd even.

All sizes:
Next rnd: Knit to marker, remove marker, place next 11 [13, 15, 17, 19] sts on waste yarn for thumb, remove marker, CO 1 st, work in patt to end of rnd. 47 [51, 57, 61, 67] sts.

Hand
Work 3 [3, 4, 5] rnds even, maintaining 2x1 Mock Cable Rib on back of hand and St st over palm. Make a note of the last patt rnd worked.
Next rnd: K15 [18, 18, 22, 22], pm for new beg of rnd.
Flap set-up rnd 1: (Kfb) 34 [36, 42, 42, 48] times (removing old marker when you come to it), knit to end.
Flap set-up rnd 2: (Place next st on waste yarn, k1) 34 [36, 42, 42, 48] times, knit to end. The 34 [36, 42, 42, 48] sts on waste yarn will be used to knit the flap later. Make sure the held sts/waste yarn are on the outside of the mitten. 47 [51, 57, 61, 67] sts rem on needles.
Work 6 [8, 9, 11, 12] rnds even, maintaining 2x1 Mock Cable Rib over 30 [30, 36, 36, 42] sts on back of hand and St st over palm.

Edging
Work as for Right Mitten.

Flap
Work as for Right Mitten.

Thumb
Work as for Right Mitten EXCEPT work Thumb Hole as foll:
Rnd 1: BO 4 [4, 4, 4, 5] sts, p8 [10, 12, 14, 15].
Rnd 2: Use backward loop method to CO 4 [4, 4, 4, 5] sts, p8 [10, 12, 14, 15].

FINISHING
Weave in all loose ends, making sure to close gaps at base of thumb. Block as desired.

ABOUT THE DESIGNER
Laura love love LOVES to knit and works full time for herself at Nelkin Designs (www.nelkindesigns.com). Between work, designing, publishing, and traveling to teach there aren't many hours in the day left, so the rest of her time is spent plotting to take LONG vacations with her family so she can play and knit some more! Laura can be found on Ravelry as LauraNelkin, and has an active group there, Nelkin Designs. Please join in—the more the merrier!

ACANTHA
BY LAURA PATTERSON

DIFFICULTY
INTERMEDIATE

Acantha was a minor character in Greek mythology. In one version of the story, Acantha was a woman who refused Apollo's advances. In another version, Acantha was a man who returned Apollo's advances.

As in the story, these mitts can take on whatever character suits your desires. Worked from the cuff towards the fingers, this pattern can be used as wrist-warming cuffs, fingerless mitts, or full mittens.

SIZES
S [M, L, 1X] (shown in size S)

FINISHED MEASUREMENTS
Hand/wrist circumference: 4.75 [6, 7.25, 8.5]"/12 [15, 18.5, 21.5]cm

MATERIALS
Cephalopod Yarns Buggal [80% merino wool, 10% cashmere, 10% nylon; 412yds/377m per 113g skein]; color: Dragon Millipede; 1 skein

Set of US #2/2.75mm dpns
Stitch markers
Waste yarn
Yarn needle

GAUGE
33 sts/52 rows = 4"/10cm in stitch patt

PATTERN
CUFFS
Loosely CO 40 [50, 60, 70] sts, pm and join to work in the round. Work k1, p1 rib for 0.5"/1.5cm. Work Rnds 1-28 of chart. Next rnd: Work k1, p1 rib for 0.5"/1.5cm. Next rnd: *P4, right twist purl, p4; rep from * to end. Work k1, p1 rib for 0.5"/1.5cm. BO loosely in rib.

FINGERLESS MITTS (both alike)
Loosely CO 40 [50, 60, 70] sts, pm and join to work in the round. Work k1, p1 rib for 0.5"/1.5cm. Work even following chart until mitt measures approx. 3"/7.5cm from CO, ending with Rnd 5 of chart.

Thumb gusset:
Rnd 1: Work 9 sts in patt, m1, pm, k2, pm, m1, work in patt to end.
Rnd 2: Work in patt to marker, sm, k2, sm, work in patt to end.
Rnd 3: Work in patt to marker, sm, (kfb) twice, sm, work in patt to end. 4 sts between the markers.
Rnd 4: Work in patt to marker, sm, knit to next marker, sm, work in patt to end.
Rnd 5: Work in patt to marker, sm, kfb, knit to 1 st before next marker, kfb, sm, work in patt to end. 2 sts inc'd.
Rep Rnds 4-5 [7, 9, 11] more times, until there are 16 [20, 24, 28] sts between the markers, then Rep Rnd 4 only until mitt measures 5 [5.5, 6, 6.5]"/12.5 [14, 15, 16.5]cm from cast on.
Next rnd: Work in patt to marker, remove marker, place next 16 [20, 24, 28] sts on waste yarn for thumb, remove marker, work in patt to end. 40 [50, 60, 70] sts rem.**

Hand:
Work even following chart until mitt measures approx. 6.5 [6.5, 7.5, 7.5]"/16.5 [16.5, 19, 19]cm from CO, ending with Rnd 16 [16, 28, 28] of chart.

Sizes –[–, L, 1X] only:
Next rnd: *P4, right twist purl, p4; rep from * to end.

All sizes:
Work k1, p1 rib for 0.5"/1.5cm. BO loosely in rib.

Thumb:
Transfer 16 [20, 24, 28] sts from waste yarn to needles. Join yarn, knit across these sts, pm, pick up and knit 3 sts from base of thumb. 19 [23, 27, 31] sts.
Next rnd: Knit.
Next rnd: Sl2, k1, p2sso, knit to 1 st before end, sl1, remove marker, return slipped st to left needle, pm. 17 [21, 25, 29] sts.
Next rnd: Sl2, k1, p2sso, knit to end. 15 [19, 23, 27] sts.
Work even in St st for 0.5"/1.5cm, or desired length.
Next rnd: *K1, p1; rep from * to last st, k1.
Rep last rnd until ribbing measures 0.5"/1.5cm. BO loosely in rib.

19

MITTENS (both alike)
Work as for Fingerless Mitts to *.

Hand:
Work even following chart until mitt measures approx. 8.25 [9.25, 10.25, 11]"/21 [23.5, 26, 28]cm, or 0.5 [0.75, 0.75, 1]"/1.5 [2, 2, 2.5] cm less than desired finished length, ending with an even-numbered rnd of chart.

Shape top:
Rnd 1: Work 10 sts in patt, pm, work 20 [25, 30, 35] sts in patt, pm, work 10 [15, 20, 25] sts in patt to end of rnd.
Rnd 2: (Work in patt to 3 sts before marker, k2tog, k1, sm, k1, ssk) twice, work in patt to end. 4 sts dec'd.
Rep Rnd 2 4 [5, 6, 7] more times. 20 [26, 32, 38] sts rem. Cut yarn leaving a 12"/30cm tail. Divide rem sts evenly over two needles and graft closed.

Thumb
Transfer 16 [20, 24, 28] sts from waste yarn to needles. Join yarn, knit across these sts, pm, pick up and knit 3 sts from base of thumb. 19 [23, 27, 31] sts.
Rnd 1: Knit to marker, sm, sl2, k1, p2sso. 17 [21, 25, 29] sts rem.
Rnd 2: Knit to 1 st before marker, sl1, remove marker, return slipped st to left needle, pm, sl2, k1, p2sso. 15 [19, 23, 27] sts rem.
Rep Rnd 2 on every third rnd 1 [1, 2, 2] more times. 13 [17, 19, 23] sts rem.

Work even until thumb measures 1 [1.25, 1.5, 1.75]"/2.5 [3, 3.5, 4.5] cm, or desired finished length less 0.25"/0.5cm.

Sizes - [M, -1X] only:
Rep Rnd 2. - [15, -, 21] sts rem.

Sizes S [-, L, -] only:
K2tog, knit to end. 12 [-, 18, -] sts rem.

All sizes:
Next rnd: *K1, k2tog; rep from * to end. 8 [10, 12, 14] sts rem.
Next rnd: *K2tog; rep from * to end. 4 [5, 6, 7] sts rem.
Break yarn, thread through rem sts and pull tight to close.

FINISHING
Weave in ends. Wash and block.

ABOUT THE DESIGNER
Mostly self-taught, Laura learned to knit and crochet while in grammar school. After taking a couple of classes at her LYS 18 years later, she finally learned to read a pattern. Not wanting to rush into anything, it took another 20 years before she began to design. Find Laura online at www.fiberdreams.com and as FiberDreams on Ravelry.

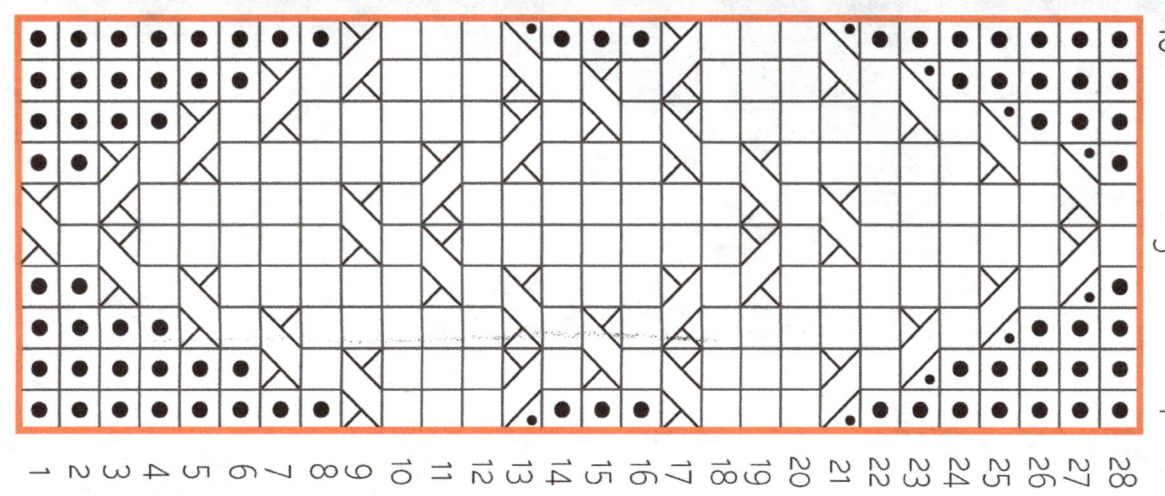

☐ knit

• purl

☐ pattern repeat

⟋⟍ Right Twist: slip 2 sts tog kwise to right needle. Insert left needle through both slipped sts from left to right, remove right needle. (K1tbl) twice.

⟍⟋ Left Twist: slip 2 sts kwise to right needle, one at a time. Insert left needle through both slipped sts from right to left, remove right needle. (K1tbl) twice.

⟋⟍• Right Twist Purl: slip 2 sts tog kwise to right needle. Insert left needle through both slipped sts from left to right, remove right needle. K1tbl, p1.

•⟍⟋ Left Twist Purl: slip 2 sts kwise to right needle, one at a time. Insert left needle through both slipped sts from right to left, remove right needle. P1, k1tbl.

BANGLES

BY REBECCA BLAIR

DIFFICULTY: INTERMEDIATE

Bangles are lightweight gloves that are plain, with the exception of their extravagant cuffs. The cuff pattern is very simple—bands of stockinette stitch alternate with reverse stockinette—but the effect is dramatic, like a stack of narrow bracelets for each wrist. A glittery silk blend yarn adds to the jeweled effect.

SIZES
S [M, L] (shown in size S)

FINISHED MEASUREMENTS
Hand circumference: 6.5 [7.25, 7.75]"/17 [18, 19.5]cm

MATERIALS
Lisa Souza Cashmere Silk Fingering [55% bombyx silk, 45% cashmere; 400yds/365m per 56g skein]; color: Garnet; 1 skein

Set of US #2/2.75mm dpns
Stitch markers
Waste yarn
Yarn needle

GAUGE
33 sts/46 rnds = 4"/10cm in St st

STITCHES
Cuff Pattern (multiple of 2 sts)
Rnd 1: Purl.
Rnd 2: *Yo, p2tog; rep from * to end.
Rnd 3: Purl.
Rnds 4-6: Knit.
Rnds 7-9: Purl.
Rnds 10-12: Knit.
Rep Rnds 1-12.

PATTERN NOTES
This cashmere/silk yarn does not have a lot of memory and is prone to sagging slightly. This tendency can be counteracted by making the gloves with some negative ease, so that they stretch to fit. (For example, the 6.5" gloves stretched to fit my my 7.5" hands comfortably.) Therefore, when selecting a size, choose a size smaller than the hands the gloves are meant for.

PATTERN
GLOVE (BOTH ALIKE)
CO 56 [60, 64] sts, pm and join to work in the round. Knit 8 rnds. Work the 12 rnds of Cuff Pattern a total of 5 times (60 rnds).

Thumb gusset:
Rnd 1: K28 [30, 32], pm, m1R, k1, m1L, pm, knit to end: 3 sts between the gusset markers.
Rnds 2-3: Knit.
Rnd 4: Knit to marker, sm, m1R, knit to next marker, m1L, sm, knit to end of rnd. 2 sts inc'd between the gusset markers.
Rnds 5-6: Knit.
Rep Rnds 4-6 [7, 8] more times, until there are 19 [19, 21] sts between the markers.
Next rnd: Knit to marker, remove marker, place next 19 [19, 21] sts on waste yarn for thumb, remove second marker, using backward loop method CO 1 st over the gap, knit to end of rnd. 56 [60, 64] sts rem.

Hand:
Work in St st for 12 [12, 14] rnds, or until glove just reaches base of little finger. Remove beg-of-rnd marker.

Little finger:
Knit first 7 sts of rnd. Place next 42 [46, 50] sts on waste yarn. CO 2 sts using the backward loop method, knit last 7 sts. 16 sts rem. Work even in St st until finger measures 2.25 [2.5, 2.75]"/5.5 [6.5, 7]cm, or desired length. Next rnd: *K2, k2tog; rep from * to end. 12 sts. Next rnd: *K1, k2tog; rep from * to end. 8 sts. Next rnd: *K2tog; rep from * to end. 4 sts. Cut yarn, thread through rem sts, pull tight and fasten off.

Ring finger:
Place next 6 [7, 7] sts from each end of waste yarn onto dpn. Join yarn and knit across first 6 [7, 7] sts, CO 2 sts, k6 [7, 7], pick up and knit 4 sts from base of little finger. 18 [20, 20] sts rem. Next rnd: K14 [16, 16], ssk, k2tog, 16 [18, 18] sts rem. Work even in St st until finger measures 2.5 [2.75, 3]"/6.5 [7, 7.5]cm, or desired length.

Size S only:
Next rnd: *K2, k2tog; rep from * to end. 12 sts. Next rnd: *K1, k2tog; rep from * to end. 8 sts. Next rnd: *K2tog; rep from * to end. 4 sts.

Sizes M and L only:
Next rnd: *K1, k2tog; rep from * to end.

All sizes:
Cut yarn, thread through rem sts, pull tight and fasten off.

Middle finger:
Place next 7 [8, 9] sts from each end of waste yarn onto dpn. Join yarn and knit across first 7 [8, 9] sts, CO 2 sts, k7 [8, 9], pick up and knit 4 sts from base of ring finger. 20 [22, 24] sts rem. Next rnd: K16 [18, 20], ssk, k2tog, 18 [20, 22] sts rem. Work even in St st until finger measures 2.75 [3, 3.25]"/7 [7.5, 8]cm, or desired length.

Size S only:
Next rnd: *K1, k2tog; rep from * to end. 12 sts. Next rnd: *K2tog; rep from * to end. 6 sts.

Size M only:
Next rnd: *K2, k2tog; rep from * to end. 15 sts. Next rnd: *K1, k2tog; rep from * to end. 10 sts. Next rnd: *K2tog; rep from * to end. 5 sts.

Size L only:
Next rnd: *K1, k2tog; rep from * to last 4 sts, (k2tog) twice. 14 sts. Next rnd: *K2tog; rep from * to end. 7 sts.

All sizes:
Cut yarn, thread through rem sts, pull tight and fasten off.

Index finger:
Place rem 16 [16, 18] sts from waste yarn on dpn. Join yarn and knit across all sts, then pick up and knit 4 sts from base of middle finger. 20 [20, 22] sts rem. Next rnd: K16 [16, 18], ssk, k2tog, 18 [18, 20] sts rem. Work even in St st until finger measures 2.5 [2.75, 3]"/6.5 [7, 7.5]cm, or desired length.

Sizes S and M only:
Next rnd: *K1, k2tog; rep from * to end. 12 sts. Next rnd: *K2tog; rep from * to end. 6 sts.

Size L only:
Next rnd: *K2, k2tog; rep from * to end. 15 sts. Next rnd: *K1, k2tog; rep from * to end. 10 sts. Next rnd: *K2tog; rep from * to end. 5 sts.

All sizes:
Cut yarn, thread through rem sts, pull tight and fasten off.

Thumb:
Place 19 [19, 21] held sts for thumb on dpn. Join yarn and knit across all sts, then pick up and knit 3 sts from CO edge. 22 [22, 24] sts. Next rnd: K19 [19, 21], sl1, k2tog, psso. 20 [20, 22] sts rem. Work even in St st until thumb measures 1.75 [2, 2.25]"/4.5 [5, 5.5]cm, or desired length.

Sizes S and M only:
Next rnd: *K2, k2tog; rep from * to end. 15 sts. Next rnd: *K1, k2tog; rep from * to end. 10 sts. Next rnd: *K2tog; rep from * to end. 5 sts.

Size L only:
*K1, k2tog; rep from * to last 2 sts, (k2tog) twice. 14 sts. Next rnd: *K2tog; rep from * to end. 7 sts.

All sizes:
Cut yarn, thread through rem sts, pull tight and fasten off.

FINISHING

Weave in all ends. Use loose ends at the base of each finger to mend holes in these areas if necessary. Block gloves by soaking in lukewarm water, squeezing in a towel to remove excess water, and laying flat to dry. Trim woven-in ends after gloves are completely dry.

ABOUT THE DESIGNER

Rebecca lives and knits on the Canadian prairies. Her favorite projects are elaborate old-fashioned lace shawls and doilies, or warm winter accessories. She blogs sporadically at doiliesarestylish.blogspot.com and can be found on Ravelry as bewilderbeast.

KELLY

BY RUTH GARCIA-ALCANTUD

Knit with cashmere and a barely-there lace detail, these simple gloves are a beautiful accessory to be treasured. They feature an anatomically correct thumb gusset and ease areas for fingers, allowing movement and a better fit.

DIFFICULTY
INTERMEDIATE

SIZES
S [M, L] (shown in size M)

FINISHED MEASUREMENTS
Hand circumference: 6.25 [7, 8]"/16 [18, 20.5]cm

MATERIALS
Indigodragonfly 4ply Cashmere [100% cashmere; 192yds/175m per 50g skein]; color: Monarchy; 2 skeins

1 36-inch US #0/2mm circular needle or set of dpns, as preferred
1 36-inch US #1/2.25mm circular needle or set of dpns, as preferred
Stitch markers
Yarn needle
Waste yarn
US E/3.5mm crochet hook
Stitch holders

GAUGE
34 sts/42 rows = 4"/10cm in St st on larger needle

STITCHES
Crochet Provisional Cast On
With waste yarn and crochet hook, make a chain a few sts longer than number to be cast on. Cut yarn and fasten off. Tie a knot in the yarn tail. With knitting needle and working yarn, pick up and knit 1 st in back "bump" of each chain st until you have the required number of sts.

PATTERN NOTES
The pattern is written for working in the round on one long circular needle using the magic loop method, but any method for working in the round may be used.

The gloves feature a double cuff created by knitting the full length of the cuff with a provisional cast on, then unraveling and working the live cast on stitches with the stitches on the needle.

PATTERN
LEFT GLOVE
Cuff:
Using the crochet provisional method and smaller needle, CO 46 [50, 56] sts. Pm and join to work in the round. Work in Twisted Rib for 2"/5cm. Change to larger needle and continue in Twisted Rib until cuff measures 4"/10cm. Fold the provisional CO edge to the inside of the work, and, unraveling the waste yarn carefully, knit 2 sts together by taking one from the needle and one from the provisional CO. Continue in this manner until all sts have been worked. 46 [50, 56] sts.
Next rnd: Knit, inc 8 [10, 12] sts evenly spaced. 54 [60, 68] sts.
Set-up rnd for chart and thumb gusset: K19 [20, 22] sts, work chart patt over 6 sts, knit to last 4 [6, 8] sts, pm for thumb gusset, k2, pm for thumb gusset, k2 [4, 6]. The first 27 [30, 34] sts of the rnd are the back of the hand and the second 27 [30, 34] sts are the palm.

Thumb gusset:
Inc rnd: Work in est patts to marker, sm, mL, knit to next marker, mR, sm, work to end. 2 sts inc'd.
Rep Inc Rnd on every 3rd rnd seven more times. 18 gusset sts between the markers.
Work even until glove measures 5"/12.5cm from folded edge of cuff.

To unzip the provisional cast on, find the end of the waste yarn chain with the knot, pick out the last stitch and unravel the chain.

Twisted Rib (multiple of 2 sts)
Rnd 1: *K1 tbl, p1; rep from * to end.
Rep Rnd 1.

27

Next rnd: Work to marker, sm, place next 18 sts on waste yarn for thumb, use crochet provisional method to CO 6 [8, 10] sts, sm, work to end of rnd.
Work 1 rnd even.
Dec rnd: Work to marker, sm, ssk, knit to 2 sts before next marker, k2tog, sm, work to end. 2 sts dec'd.
Rep Dec Rnd on every 2nd rnd 1 [2, 3] more times, until 2 gusset sts rem. 54 [60, 68] sts in total. Remove gusset markers.

Hand:
Work even until glove measures 6"/15cm from folded edge of cuff, or until it reaches the base of the fingers. Divide sts over two holders, allowing first 27 [30, 34] sts of rnd for back of hand and rem 27 [30, 34] sts for palm.

Index finger:
Knit first 7 [8, 9] back-of-hand sts from holder, provisionally CO 4 sts, transfer last 7 [8, 9] sts from palm holder to needle and knit across. 18 [20, 22] sts. Work even in St st until finger measures 2.75"/7cm, or 0.25"/0.5cm less than desired length.
Next rnd: *K2tog; rep from * to end. 9 [10, 11] sts.
Knit 1 rnd.
Next rnd: K1 [0, 1], *k2tog; rep from * to end. 5 [5, 6] sts.
Knit 1 rnd.
Cut yarn, thread through rem sts, pull tight and fasten off.

Middle finger:
Knit next 7 [9, 10] back-of-hand sts from holder, provisionally CO 4 sts, transfer last 7 [9, 10] sts from palm holder to needle and knit across, unzip provisional CO from base of index finger and knit those 4 sts. 22 [26, 28] sts. Work even in St st until finger measures 3.25"/8.5cm, or 0.25"/0.5cm less than desired length.
Next rnd: *K2tog; rep from * to end. 11 [13, 14] sts.
Knit 1 rnd.
Next rnd: K1 [1, 0], *k2tog; rep from * to end. 6 [7, 7] sts.
Knit 1 rnd.
Cut yarn, thread through rem sts, pull tight and fasten off.

Third finger:
Knit next 7 [7, 8] back-of-hand sts from holder, provisionally CO 3 sts, transfer last 7 [7, 8] sts from palm holder to needle and knit across, unzip provisional CO from base of middle finger and knit those 4 sts. 21 [21, 23] sts. Work even in St st until finger measures 2.5"/6.5cm, or 0.25"/0.5cm less than desired length.
Next rnd: K1 [1, 0], *k2tog; rep from * to end. 11 [11, 12] sts.
Knit 1 rnd.
Next rnd: K1 [1, 0], *k2tog; rep from * to end. 6 [6, 6] sts.
Knit 1 rnd.
Cut yarn, thread through rem sts, pull tight and fasten off.

Little finger:
Knit rem 6 [6, 7] sts from back-of-hand holder and rem 6 [6, 7] sts from palm holder, unzip provisional CO from base of third finger and knit those 3 sts. 15 [15, 17] sts. Work even in St st until finger measures 2.25"/5.5cm, or 0.25"/0.5cm less than desired length.
Next rnd: K1, *k2tog; rep from * to end. 8 [8, 9] sts.
Knit 1 rnd.
Next rnd: K0 [0, 1], *k2tog; rep from * to end. 4 [4, 5] sts.
Cut yarn, thread through rem sts, pull tight and fasten off.

Thumb:
Transfer 18 sts from waste yarn to needle, knit across them, pm, unzip provisional CO at base of thumb and knit these 6 [8, 10] sts, pm. 24 [26, 28] sts.
Knit 1 rnd.
Dec rnd: Knit to marker, sm, ssk, knit to 2 sts before next marker, k2tog, sm. 2 sts dec'd.
Rep Dec Rnd on every rnd 1 [2, 3] more times, until 2 sts rem between the markers. 20 [22, 24] sts in total. Work even in St st until thumb measures 2.25"/5.5cm, or 0.25"/0.5cm less than desired length.
Next rnd: *K2tog; rep from * to end. 10 [11, 12] sts.
Knit 1 rnd.
Next rnd: K0 [1, 0], *k2tog; rep from * to end. 5 [6, 6] sts.
Knit 1 rnd.
Cut yarn, thread through rem sts, pull tight and fasten off.

RIGHT GLOVE
Cuff:
Using the crochet provisional method and smaller needle, CO 46 [50, 56] sts. Pm and join to work in the round. Work in Twisted Rib for 2"/5cm. Change to larger needle and continue in Twisted Rib until cuff measures 4"/10cm. Fold the provisional CO edge to the inside of the work, and, unraveling the waste yarn carefully, knit 2 sts together by taking one from the needle and one from the provisional CO. Continue in this manner until all sts have been worked. 46 [50, 56] sts.
Next rnd: Knit, inc 8 [10, 12] sts evenly spaced. 54 [60, 68] sts.
Set-up rnd for chart and thumb gusset: K2 [4, 6], pm for thumb gusset, k2, pm for thumb gusset, k25 [28, 32], work chart patt over 6 sts, knit to end. The first 27 [30, 34] sts of the rnd are the palm and the second 27 [30, 34] sts are the back of the hand.

Thumb gusset:
Work same as for Left Glove.

Hand:
Work even until glove measures 6"/15cm from folded edge of cuff, or until it reaches the base of the fingers. Divide sts over two holders, allowing first 27 [30, 34] sts of rnd for palm and rem 27 [30, 34] sts for back of hand.

Index finger:
Knit first 7 [8, 9] palm sts from holder, provisionally CO 4 sts, transfer last 7 [8, 9] sts from back-of-hand holder to needle and knit across, 18 [20, 22] sts. Work even in St st until finger measures 2.75"/7cm, or 0.25"/0.5cm less than desired length.
Next rnd: *K2tog; rep from * to end. 9 [10, 11] sts.
Knit 1 rnd.
Next rnd: K1 [0, 1], *k2tog; rep from * to end. 5 [5, 6] sts.
Knit 1 rnd.
Cut yarn, thread through rem sts, pull tight and fasten off.

Middle finger:
Knit next 7 [9, 10] palm sts from holder, provisionally CO 4 sts, transfer last 7 [9, 10] sts from back-of-hand holder to needle and knit across, unzip provisional CO from base of index finger and knit those 4 sts. 22 [26, 28] sts. Work even in St st until finger measures 3.25"/8.5cm, or 0.25"/0.5cm less than desired length.
Next rnd: *K2tog; rep from * to end. 11 [13, 14] sts.
Knit 1 rnd.
Next rnd: K1 [1, 0], *k2tog; rep from * to end. 6 [7, 7] sts.
Knit 1 rnd.
Cut yarn, thread through rem sts, pull tight and fasten off.

Third finger:
Knit next 7 [7, 8] palm sts from holder, provisionally CO 3 sts, transfer last 7 [7, 8] sts from back-of-hand holder to needle and knit across, unzip provisional CO from base of middle finger and knit those 4 sts. 21 [21, 23] sts. Work even in St st until finger measures 2.5"/6.5cm, or 0.25"/0.5cm less than desired length.
Next rnd: K1, *k2tog; rep from * to end. 11 [11, 12] sts.
Knit 1 rnd.
Next rnd: K1 [1, 0], *k2tog; rep from * to end. 6 [6, 6] sts.
Knit 1 rnd.
Cut yarn, thread through rem sts, pull tight and fasten off.

Little finger:
Knit rem 6 [6, 7] sts from palm holder and rem 6 [6, 7] sts from back-of-hand holder, unzip provisional CO from base of third finger and knit those 3 sts. 15 [15, 17] sts. Work even in St st until finger measures 2.25"/5.5cm, or 0.25"/0.5cm less than desired length.
Next rnd: K1, *k2tog; rep from * to end. 8 [8, 9] sts.
Knit 1 rnd.
Next rnd: K0 [0, 1], *k2tog; rep from * to end. 4 [4, 5] sts.
Cut yarn, thread through rem sts, pull tight and fasten off.

Thumb:
Work same as for Left Glove.

photo by Alexandra Virgiel

- ● purl
- ○ yo
- ╱ k2tog
- ╲ ssk
- ▭ pattern repeat

FINISHING
Weave in all ends. Wet block in lukewarm water. Leave to dry and feel the subtle elegance radiating from your hands.

ABOUT THE DESIGNER
Ruth plays with yarn and fiber from her home in Sussex. She loves to design with small details and bright colors to create a timeless wardrobe. Visit her on www.rockandpurl.com or on Ravelry as rockandpurl.

EQUUS QUAGGA

BY SARA PETERSON

DIFFICULTY
EXPERIENCED

These mod two-color mittens feature a zebra design on the back and a floral lattice on the palm. The outer mitten is worked in a fingering weight yarn while a slightly thinner merino/cashmere/nylon yarn is used for the lining to add a contrasting pop of color and warmth. These mittens will keep your hands in toasty luxury.

SIZES
M [L] (shown in size M)

FINISHED MEASUREMENTS
Circumference: 7.5 [8]"/19 [20.5]cm
Length: 8.75 [9.25]"/22 [23.5]cm

MATERIALS
[MC] Squoosh Fiberarts Ultra Sock [100% superwash merino wool; 400yds/366m per 100g skein]; color: Raven; 1 skein
[CC] Squoosh Fiberarts Ultra Sock; color: Natural; 1 skein
[Lining] Squoosh Fiberarts Merino Cashmere Lace [80% superwash merino wool, 10% cashmere, 10% nylon; 570yds/521m per 113g skein]; color: Water; 1 skein

1 32-inch US #2/2.75mm circular needle for size M
1 32-inch US #3/3.25mm circular needle for size L
Stitch marker
Yarn needle
Waste yarn
US E/3.5mm crochet hook

GAUGE
34 sts/36 rows = 4"/10cm in stranded St st on US #2/2.75mm needle with MC/CC for size M
32 sts/46 rows = 4"/10cm in St st on US #2/2.75mm needle with Lining yarn for size M
32 sts/34 rows = 4"/10cm in stranded St st on US #3/3.25mm needle with MC/CC for size L
29 sts/40 rows = 4"/10cm in St st on US #3/3.25mm needle with Lining yarn for size L

STITCHES
Crochet Provisional Cast On
With waste yarn and crochet hook, make a chain a few sts longer than number to be cast on. Cut yarn and fasten off. Tie a knot in the yarn tail. With knitting needle and working yarn, pick up and knit 1 st in back "bump" of each chain st until you have the required number of sts.

To unzip the provisional cast on, find the end of the waste yarn chain with the knot, pick out the last stitch and unravel the chain.

PATTERN NOTES
The mittens are worked from cuff to tip, beginning with a provisional cast on. After the outer mitten has been worked, the provisional cast-on stitches are unzipped and the lining is worked from cuff to tip.

Pattern assumes you are working in the round using the magic loop method on a long circular needle.

PATTERN
RIGHT MITTEN - OUTER
Using crochet provisional method, CO 64 sts with MC. Pm and join to work in the round. Purl 1 rnd. Knit 1 rnd.

Begin working charts as foll: Work Right Hand chart across first 33 sts, work Palm chart over next 31 sts. Continue as set through Rnd 9 of charts.

On Rnd 10, begin working thumb gusset: Work Right Hand chart over 33 sts, work Thumb Gusset chart, work Palm chart over 31 sts. Continue as set through end of Thumb Gusset chart—Rnd 37 of Hand and Palm charts. On Rnd 38, work Right Hand chart over 33 sts, slip the 27 gusset sts to waste yarn, work Palm chart over 31 sts. 64 sts rem.

31

Work even following charts through Rnd 79. 16 sts rem. Divide sts evenly over two needles and graft top of mitten closed using MC.

Thumb
Transfer 27 thumb sts to needle. Work Rnd 1 of Thumb Decrease chart, picking up and knitting 1 st with MC at base of thumb. 28 sts.
Rep Rnd 1 of Thumb Decrease chart until thumb measures 1.5 [1.75]"/4 [4.5]cm, or desired length minus 0.5"/1.5cm.
Work Thumb Decrease chart Rnds 2-7. Cut MC and CC. Thread tails through rem 4 sts with yarn needle. Pull tight to close.

Weave in ends, wash and block outer mitten.

RIGHT MITTEN - LINING
Unzip provisional CO and place these 64 sts on needle. Arrange sts so that rnds begin on the thumb side, and there are 32 sts on each needle.
With lining yarn, work in St st for 1 [1.25]"/2.5 [3]cm.

Thumb gusset:
Rnd 1: M1R, pm, knit to end.
Rnd 2: Knit.
Rnd 3: M1L, knit to marker, m1R, sm, knit to end. 2 sts inc'd.
Rep Rnds 2-3 twelve more times, then Rnd 2 once more. 27 sts between the markers.
Next rnd: Slip 27 sts to waste yarn, remove marker, knit to end. 64 sts rem.

Work even in St st until lining measures 7 [7.5]"/18 [19]cm.

Shape top:
Rnd 1: *K1, ssk, knit to last 3 sts on needle, k2tog, k1; rep from * for second needle. 4 sts dec'd.
Rnd 2: Knit.
Rep Rnds 1-2 thirteen more times. 8 sts rem. Cut yarn, thread tail through rem sts with yarn needle. Pull tight to close.

Thumb
Transfer 27 thumb sts to needle. Knit 1 rnd, picking up and knitting 1 st from base of thumb. 28 sts. (There should be 14 sts on each needle.)

Work in St st until thumb measures 1.5 [1.75]"/4 [4.5]cm, or desired length minus 0.5"/1.5cm.
Rnd 1: *Ssk, knit to last 2 sts on needle, k2tog; rep from * for second needle. 4 sts dec'd.
Rep Rnd 1 five more times. 4 sts rem. Cut yarn. Thread tails through rem sts with yarn needle. Pull tight to close.

LEFT MITTEN - OUTER
Using crochet provisional method, CO 64 sts with MC. Pm and join to work in the round. Purl 1 rnd. Knit 1 rnd.

Begin working charts as foll: Work Left Hand chart across first 33 sts, work Palm chart over next 31 sts. Continue as set through Rnd 9 of charts.

On Rnd 10, begin working thumb gusset: Work Left Hand chart over 33 sts, work Palm chart over 31 sts, work Thumb Gusset chart. Continue as set through end of Thumb Gusset chart—Rnd 37 of Hand and Palm charts. On Rnd 38, work Left Hand chart over 33 sts, work Palm chart over 31 sts, slip the 27 thumb gusset sts to waste yarn. 64 sts rem.
Work even following charts through Rnd 79. 16 sts rem.
Divide sts evenly over two needles and graft top of mitten closed using MC.

Thumb
Work as for Right Mitten.

LEFT MITTEN - LINING
Work as for Right Mitten - Lining.

FINISHING
Weave in ends, closing any holes or gaps with yarn tails. Wash and block.

ABOUT THE DESIGNER
Sara lives and works in Rochester, NY, with her husband, her dog, and three cats. Every day she works towards her dream of living on a small fiber farm. Her work can be found at http://www.knottygnome.com and she is on Ravelry as knottygnome.

PALM CHART

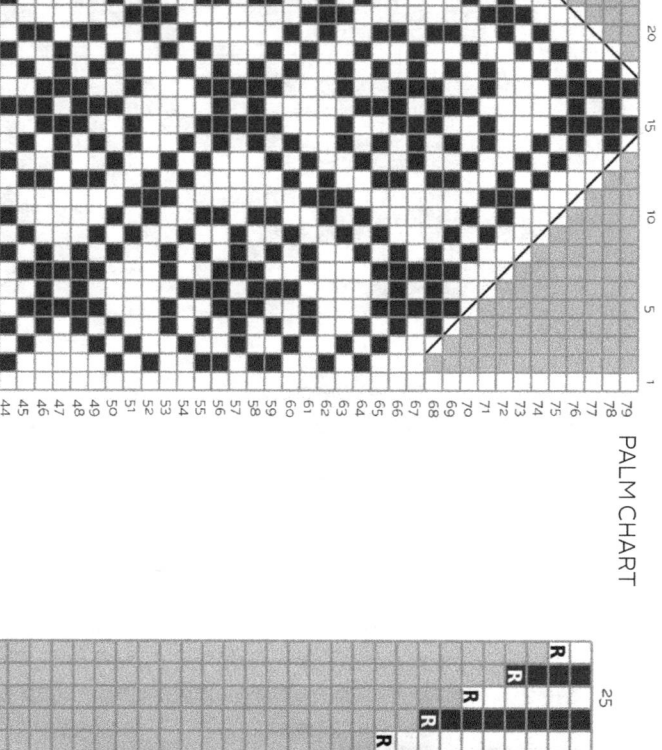

THUMB GUSSET CHART

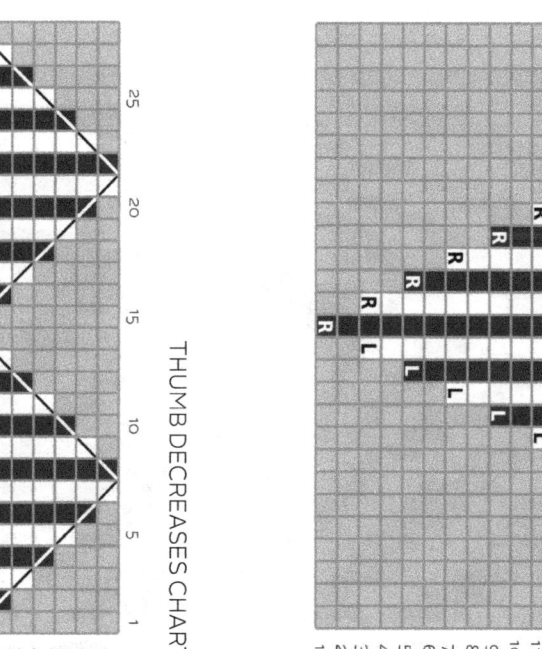

THUMB DECREASES CHART

LEGEND FOR ALL EQUUS QUAGGA CHARTS

- ☐ knit with CC
- ■ knit with MC
- ╲ k2tog with CC
- ╲ k2tog with MC
- ╱ ssk with CC
- ╲ ssk with MC
- L mL with CC
- **L** mL with MC
- R mR with CC
- **R** mR with MC
- ▨ no stitch

33

ASYLUM HILL
BY SARAH EYRE

These mittens were inspired by a set of hinges on a church door in Asylum Hill in Hartford, Connecticut. I was driving through the neighborhood while visiting my friend Chion Wolf and suddenly called out, "Pull over, pull over! I need to take pictures of those doors!" Luckily, we're both strange and unflappable women, and she didn't mind at all. The lovely twists of cast iron were absolutely hypnotizing and clearly needed to be knitwear.

DIFFICULTY
EXPERIENCED

SIZE
One size

FINISHED MEASUREMENTS
Hand circumference: 8"/20.5cm
Total length: 9.25"/23.5cm

MATERIALS
[MC] Dragonfly Fibers Djinni Sock [80% superwash merino wool, 10% cashmere, 10% nylon; 420 yds/384m per 113g skein]; color Velvet Underground (dark blue); 1 skein
[CC] Cephalopod Yarns Skinny Bugga! [80% superwash merino wool, 10% cashmere, 10% nylon; 424 yds/387m per 113g skein]; color Starry Night Cracker (blue-green); 1 skein

Two US #1/2.25mm circular needles or set of dpns, as preferred
Yarn needle
Stitch markers
Waste yarn

GAUGE
32 sts/36 rows = 4"/10cm in stranded colorwork

PATTERN
LEFT MITTEN
With MC, CO 64 sts, divide evenly over two circular needles or 3 or 4 dpns, and join to work in the round. Work k2, p2 rib for 1.5"/3.5cm. Set up rnd: Work Rnd 1 of Palm Chart over 32 sts, pm, work Rnd 1 of Back of Hand Chart over 32 sts. Continue as set through Rnd 28 of charts.
Set up for thumb on next rnd: Work Rnd 29 of Palm Chart for 21 sts, knit the next 8 sts with waste yarn, slip the waste yarn sts back to the left needle and knit them again following charted patt, continue in established patt to end of rnd. Work even through Rnd 70 of charts. 28 sts rem.
Divide sts evenly over two needles and graft top of mitten closed using MC.

Thumb:
Remove waste yarn and place 8 live sts from bottom and 8 live sts from top of resulting opening on needles. Work in the round following Thumb Chart through Rnd 24. 4 sts rem. Cut yarn, thread through rem sts, pull closed and fasten off.

RIGHT MITTEN
With MC, CO 64 sts, divide evenly over two circular needles or 3 or 4 dpns, and join to work in the round. Work k2, p2 rib for 1.5"/3.5cm. Set up rnd: Work Rnd 1 of Back of Hand Chart over 32 sts, knit the next 8 sts with waste yarn, slip the waste yarn sts back to the left needle and knit them again following charted patt, continue in established patt to end of rnd.
Work even through Rnd 70 of charts. 28 sts rem.
Divide sts evenly over two needles and graft top of mitten closed using MC.

Thumb:
Work as for Left Mitten.

FINISHING
Weave in ends and wet block.

ABOUT THE DESIGNER
Sarah Eyre owns Cephalopod Yarns (cephalopodyarns.com) with her husband, Sam Taylor. A dyer, designer, writer, and teacher, she is also a terrible banjo player and a full-time Professional Dilettante. She writes at www.onmytiptoes.com.

37

BACK OF HAND CHART

LEGEND FOR ALL
ASYLUM HILL CHARTS

knit with CC
knit with MC
k2tog with MC
ssk with MC
no stitch

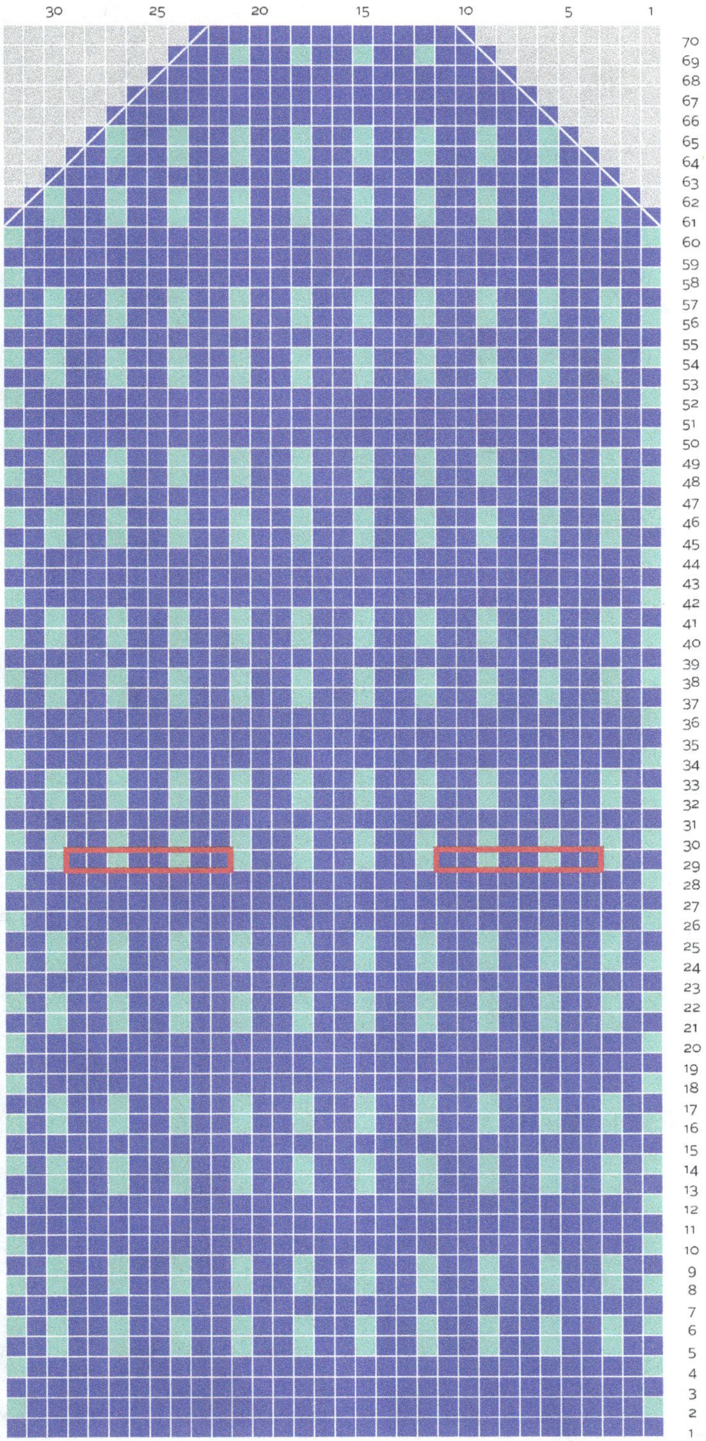

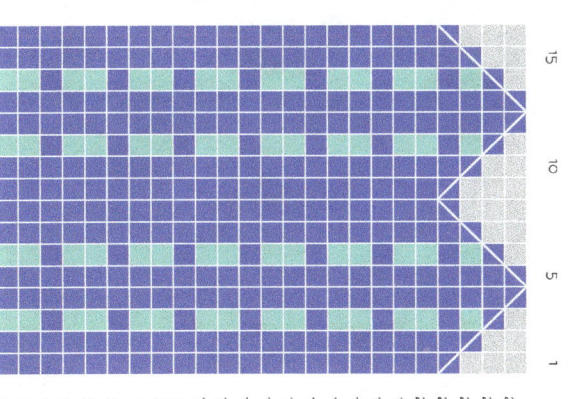

PALM CHART
(Red boxes indicate thumb gusset placement.)

THUMB CHART

CABLE TILT
BY SARAH WILSON

These fingerless mitts will keep you on your toes, from the intricate, biased cable that crosses on both right and wrong sides to the unusual shaping in the twisted rib, but the payoff is spectacular with an accessory that will leave people saying, "Wow!"

DIFFICULTY
EXPERIENCED

SIZE
One size fits most. Adjustable by leaving buttons undone as needed.

FINISHED MEASUREMENTS
Width: 5.75"/14.5cm (unbuttoned and unstretched)
Length: 10"/25.5cm

MATERIALS
Squoosh Fiberarts Rapture [75% superwash merino 15% silk, 10% cashmere; 370yds/338m per 113g skein]; color: Fresh Cut; 1 skein
US #1.5/2.5mm straight needles
Set of US #1.5/2.5mm dpns
24 1/4"/6mm shank buttons
Stitch markers
Cable needle
Waste yarn
Yarn needle
Sewing needle and matching thread

GAUGE
50 sts/46 rows = 4"/10cm in Twisted 1x1 Rib, unstretched

STITCHES
For special stitches, see chart key on page 45.

Twisted 1x1 Rib (multiple of 2 sts)
Row 1 (RS): *K1 tbl, p1; rep from * to end.
Row 2 (WS): *K1, p1 tbl; rep from * to end.
Rep Rows 1-2.

PATTERN NOTES
In this pattern, yarn overs are used as one method of increasing. However, please note that on the following row, you will be working these stitches through the back loop, thereby closing the yarn over hole.

PATTERN
LEFT MITT
With straight needles, CO 74 sts.
Row 1 (WS): K3, p1 tbl, pm, (p1 tbl, k1) 4 times, p1 tbl, (p1 tbl, k1) 4 times, p1 tbl, pm, *p1 tbl, k1; rep from * to last 4 sts, p1 tbl, k3.
Row 2 (RS): K3, *k1 tbl, p1; rep from * to 1 st before marker, k1 tbl, sm, (k1 tbl, p1) 4 times, k1 tbl, (k1 tbl, p1) 4 times, k1 tbl, sm, *k1 tbl, p1; rep from * to last 4 sts, k1 tbl, k3.
Row 3: K3, p1 tbl, sm, (p1 tbl, k1) 4 times, p1 tbl, (p1 tbl, k1) 4 times, p1 tbl, sm, *p1 tbl, k1; rep from * to last 4 sts, p1 tbl, k3.
Rows 4-7: Rep Rows 2-3.
Row 8 (RS): K3, *k1 tbl, p1; rep from * to 3 sts before marker, k1 tbl, p2tog, sm, (k1 tbl, p1) twice, k1 tbl, c2 over 2 left, c2 over 2 right, k1 tbl, (p1, k1 tbl) twice, sm, c2 over 1 left p, p4, c2 over 1 right p, (k1, p1 tbl) twice, sm, *k1, p1 tbl; rep from * to last 3 sts, k3.
Row 9 (WS): K3, p1 tbl, k1 tbl, sm, (p1 tbl, k1) twice, c2 over 1 left p, p4, c2 over 1 right p, (k1, p1 tbl) twice, sm, *k1, p1 tbl; rep from * to last 3 sts, k3.
Work Rows 1-24 of Chart A twice, then Rows 1-22 of chart once more. 79 rows in total from CO. With RS facing, sts should be arranged on needle as foll (reading right to left): 16 sts, marker, 18 sts, marker, 40 sts.

Thumb gusset:
Set-up row (RS, Row 1 of Chart B): K3, *k1 tbl, p1; rep from * to 3 sts before marker, k1 tbl, p2tog, sm, (k1 tbl, p1) twice, k1 tbl, pm for gusset, RLI, k1 tbl, LLI, pm for gusset, *p1, k1 tbl; rep from * to 2 left, c2 over 2 right, k1 tbl, (p1, k1 tbl) twice, sm, yo, k1 tbl, pm for gusset, *p1, k1 tbl; rep from * to last 3 sts, k2tog, yo, k1.
Work Rows 2-18 of Chart B once.

Next row (RS, Row 19 of Chart B): Work following chart to first gusset marker, remove marker, sl next 19 sts to waste yarn, remove marker, work following chart to end. 73 sts rem. Work Rows 20-26 of Chart B once, then work Rows 27-28 a total of three times. 72 sts in patt. BO all sts in patt.

Thumb:
With RS facing using a dpn, join yarn, pick up and knit 7 sts along open edge of thumb opening, pm for beg of rnd. Transfer 19 held sts to dpn. 26 sts.
Rnds 1-7: *P1, k1 tbl; rep from * to end.
BO all sts loosely in pattern.

RIGHT MITT
With straight needles, CO 74 sts.
Row 1 (WS): K3, (p1 tbl, k1) 24 times, p1 tbl, pm, (p1 tbl, k1) 4 times, p1 tbl, (p1 tbl, k1) 4 times, p1 tbl, sm, p1 tbl, k3.
Row 2 (RS): K3, k1 tbl, sm, (k1 tbl, p1) 4 times, k1 tbl, (k1 tbl, p1) 4 times, k1 tbl, sm, *k1 tbl, p1; rep from * to last 4 sts, k1 tbl, k3.
Row 3: K3, *p1 tbl, k1; rep from * to 1 st before marker, p1 tbl, sm, (p1 tbl, k1) 4 times, p1 tbl, (p1 tbl, k1) 4 times, p1 tbl, sm, p1 tbl, k3.
Rows 4-7: Rep Rows 2-3.
Row 8 (RS): K2tog, yo, k1, k1 tbl, yo, sm, (k1 tbl, p1) twice, k1 tbl, c2 over 2 left, c2 over 2 right, k1 tbl, (p1, k1 tbl) twice, sm, p2tog, *k1 tbl, p1; rep from * to last 4 sts, k1 tbl, k3.
Row 9 (WS): K3, *p1 tbl, k1; rep from * to marker, sm, (p1 tbl, k1) twice, c2 over 1 left purl, p4, c2 over 1 right purl, (k1, p1 tbl) twice, k1 tbl, p1 tbl, k3.
Work Rows 1-24 of Chart C twice, then Rows 1-22 of chart once more. 79 rows in total from CO. With RS facing, sts should be arranged on needle as foll (reading right to left): 40 sts, marker, 18 sts, marker, 16 sts.

Thumb gusset:
Set-up row (RS, Row 1 of Chart D): K2tog, yo, k1, *k1 tbl, p1; rep from * to 3 sts before marker, pm for gusset, RLI, k1 tbl, LLI, pm for gusset, p1, k1 tbl, yo, sm, (k1 tbl, p1) twice, k1 tbl, c2 over 2 left, c2 over 2 right, k1 tbl, (p1, k1 tbl) twice, sm, p2tog, *k1 tbl, p1; rep from * to last 4 sts, k1 tbl, k3.
Work Rows 2-18 of Chart D once.
Next row (RS, Row 19 of Chart D): Work following chart to gusset marker, remove marker, sl next 9 sts to waste yarn, remove marker, work following chart to end. 73 sts.
Work Rows 20-26 of Chart D once, then work Rows 27-28 a total of three times. 72 sts in patt.
BO all sts in patt.

Thumb:
Work same as left mitt.

FINISHING
Steam block lightly to shape. Weave in all ends. With sewing thread, attach buttons.

ABOUT THE DESIGNER
Sarah Wilson is The Sexy Knitter. Find her on the web at www.sexyknitter.com, or on Ravelry, Twitter, Pinterest, Etsy and Facebook as TheSexyKnitter.

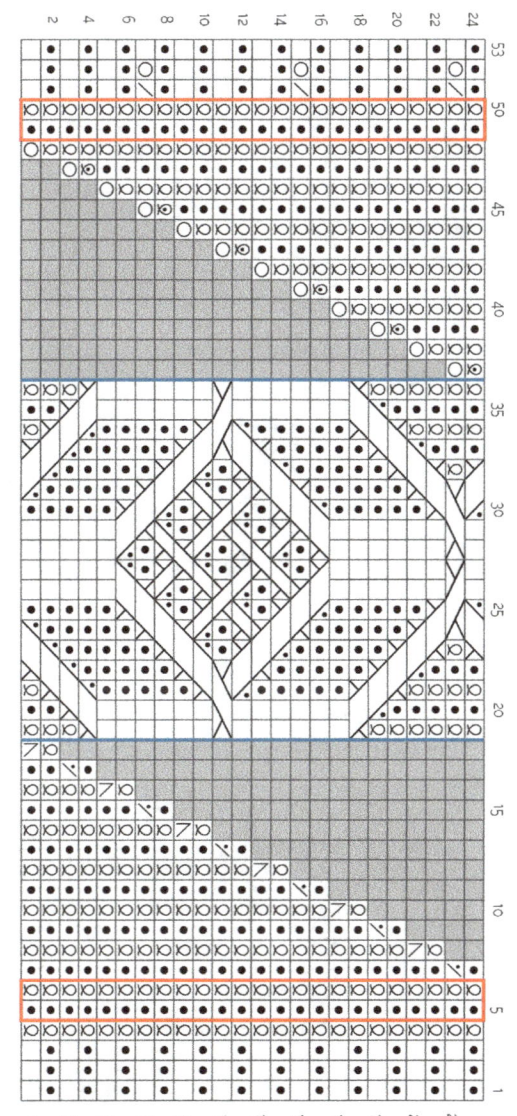

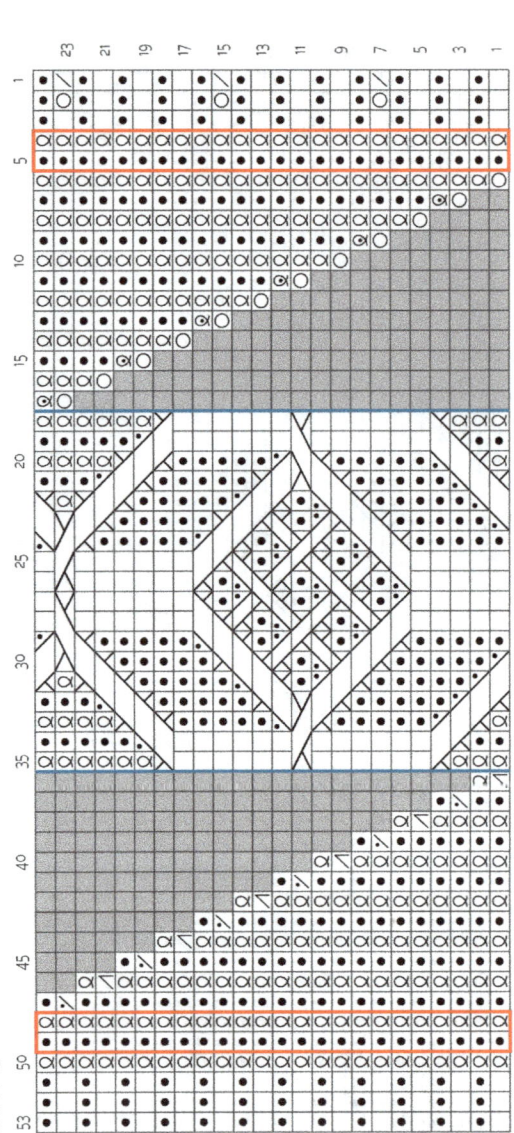

CHART C

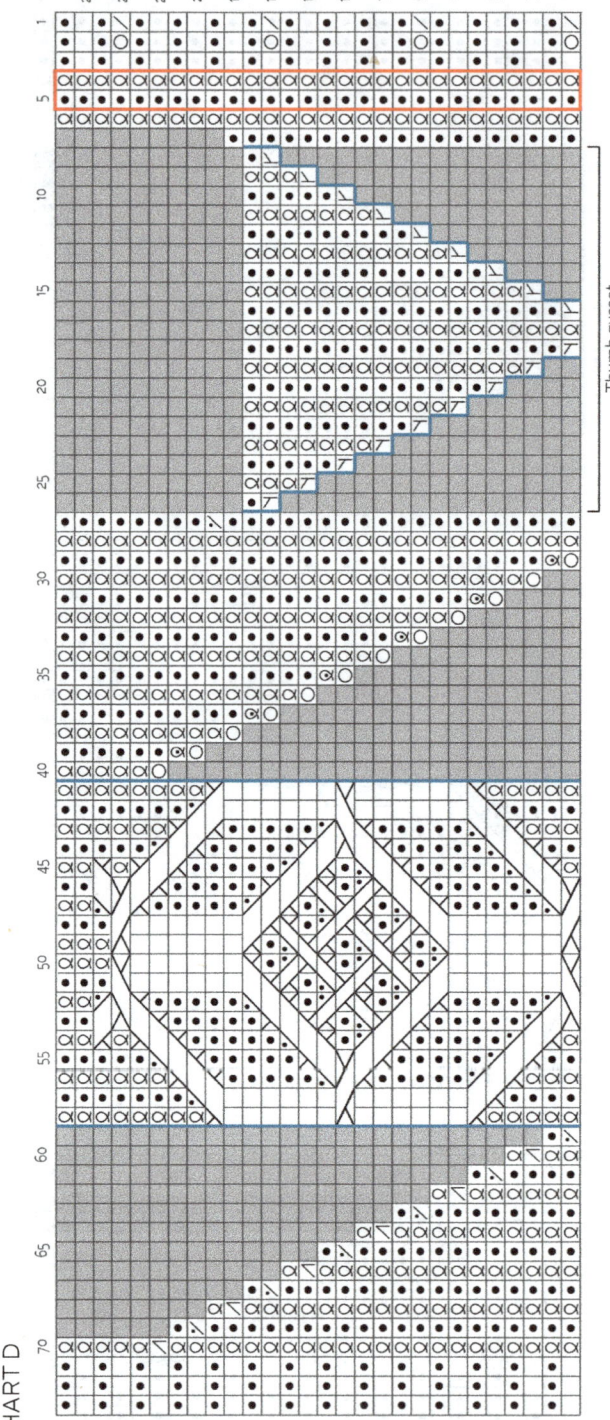

CHART D

LEGEND FOR ALL CABLE TILT CHARTS

☐ RS: Knit
  WS: Purl

● RS: Purl
  WS: Knit

ℚ RS: Knit tbl
  WS: Purl tbl

ℚ WS: Knit tbl

○ RS: Yarn over

⅄ RLI (right lifted inc)
  RS: Use the right ndl to pick up the back of the st below the next st on the left ndl. Place it on the left ndl, then knit into it.

⅄ LLI (left lifted inc)
  RS: Use the left ndl to pick up the back of the st two rows below the st just knit on right ndl, then knit into it.

⋅ RS: P2tog
  WS: K2tog

╲ RS: K2tog

∧ Ldec (twisted left dec)
  RS: Sl1 pwise wyib; sl1 kwise wyib; transfer both sts back to left ndl and k2tog tbl.

∧ Rdec (twisted left dec)
  RS: Sl1 pwise wyib; sl1 pwise tbl wyib; transfer both sts back to left ndl and k2tog.

▪ No Stitch

⋋⋌ C1 over 1 left p
  WS: Sl1 to CN, hold in front. P1, k1 from CN.

⋋⋌ C1 over 1 right p
  WS: Sl1 to CN, hold in back. K1, p1 from CN.

⋋⋌ C2 over 1 left p
  WS: Sl1 to CN, hold in front. P2, k2 from CN.

⋋⋌ C2 over 1 right p
  RS: Sl1 to CN, hold in back. K2, p1 from CN.
  WS: Sl2 to CN, hold in back. K1, p2 from CN.

⋋⋌ C1 over 1 left
  RS: Sl1 to CN, hold in front. K1, k1 from CN.

⋋⋌ C1 over 1 right
  RS: Sl1 to CN, hold in back. K1, k1 from CN.

⋋⋌ C2 over 1 left
  RS: Sl1 to CN, hold in front. K1, k2 from CN.
  WS: Sl1 to CN, hold in back. P2, p1 from CN.

⋋⋌ C2 over 1 right
  RS: Sl2 to CN, hold in back. K2, k1 from CN.
  WS: Sl2 to CN, hold in front. P1, p2 from CN.

⋋⋌ C2 over 2 left
  RS: Sl2 to CN, hold in front. K2, k2 from CN.

⋋⋌ C2 over 2 right
  RS: Sl2 to CN, hold in back. K2, k2 from CN.

☐ Pattern repeat

— Stitch marker

EMPYREAN
BY SHARON FULLER

DIFFICULTY: INTERMEDIATE

Empyrean (df.): The apparent surface of the imaginary sphere on which celestial bodies appear to be projected.

Create your own heavenly projection with these gloves, beautifully decorated with beaded diamonds on the back and palm.

SIZES
S [M, L] (shown in size M)

FINISHED MEASUREMENTS
Hand circumference: 6 [6.5, 7]"/15 [16.5, 18]cm
These gloves are designed to be worn with about 1"/2.5cm negative ease.

MATERIALS
Yarn Love Elizabeth Bennet [65% superwash merino, 20% bamboo, 15% silk; 195 yds/178m per 50g skein]; color: Into the Deep; 1 [2, 2] skeins
Note: You may be able to squeeze size M out of a single skein if you unravel your gauge swatch.

1 32-inch US #0/2mm circular needle
1 32-inch US #1.5/2.5mm circular needle
Japanese glass seed beads size 8/0; color: silver matte; 170 [176, 182] beads (or 114 [120, 126] if beading is done only on cuffs and back of hand)
US #11/1.1mm steel crochet hook for beading
US E/3.5mm crochet hook for provisional cast on
Waste yarn
Stitch markers
Yarn needle

GAUGE
32 sts/44 rnds = 4"/10cm in St st on larger needles, blocked.
48 sts/40 rnds = 4"/10cm in chart patt on larger needles, blocked.

STITCHES
Crochet Provisional Cast On
With waste yarn and crochet hook, make a chain a few sts longer than number to be cast on. Cut yarn and fasten off. Tie a knot in the yarn tail. With knitting needle and working yarn, pick up and knit 1 st in back "bump" of each chain st until you have the required number of sts.

To unzip the provisional cast on, find the end of the waste yarn chain with the knot, pick out the last stitch and unravel the chain.

Purl Cast On
The purl cast on is exactly the same as the knitted-on cast on, except that it is done in purl. This cast on is recommended for the extra thumb sts because the cast on sts are easy to pick up.
*Purl first st on the left needle, place new st back on left needle; rep from * until desired number of sts have been cast on.

Place Bead
Put bead on steel crochet hook, then use the hook to pull the next stitch through the bead. Put the stitch on the right needle.

PATTERN NOTES
The pattern is written for working in the round on one long circular needle using the magic loop method.

PATTERN
RIGHT GLOVE
Picot Cuff:
Using the crochet provisional method and smaller needle, CO 58 [64, 70] sts. Leave a tail at least 20"/51cm long for sewing up the hem later. Arrange sts so there are an even number on each needle tip. Join to work in the round, being careful not to twist. Knit 6 rnds.
Picot rnd: *Yo, k2tog; rep from * to end.

47

Change to larger needle. Knit 1 rnd
Bead rnd: *K1, place bead; rep from * to end.
Next rnd: Sl1, knit to end.
Knit 5 rnds.

Arrange sts so you have 30 [33, 36] sts for back of hand on first needle tip, and 28 [31, 34] sts for palm on second needle tip.

Wrist and lower hand:
The increases and decreases in the chart keep the ribbing on the back of the hand straight and create a bit of a gusset for the thumb. Not much shaping is needed for the gusset because space for the thumb grows naturally as the work is released from the ribbing.

Work charted patterns as follows:
Back of hand: K5 [7, 8], pm, work Right Back chart, pm, k7 [8, 10].
Palm: K4 [5, 7], pm, work Right Palm chart, pm, k6 [8, 9].

When all 45 rnds of charts are complete, 56 [62, 68] sts remain and each needle tip holds 28 [31, 34] sts.

Middle of hand and thumb hole:
Work 3 [6, 9] rnds even or until glove measures 2.5 [2.75, 3]"/6.5 [7, 7.5]cm from middle of the charted patt (approx. Rnd 23 on chart). If a fitting is possible, have the recipient try on the glove to confirm that this is the correct place to start the thumb, and add or subtract rounds accordingly.

Next rnd: K21 [23, 25], place next 14 [16, 18] sts on waste yarn for thumb, turn work so WS is facing, use purl CO method to CO 8 sts, turn work so RS is facing, knit to end of rnd. 50 [54, 58] sts rem.

Rearrange sts so you have 25 [27, 29] on each needle tip.
Knit 3 rnds.
Next rnd: Knit to last 3 sts on first needle, k2tog, k1; on second needle, k1, ssk, knit to end. 2 sts dec'd.
Rep the last 4 rnds twice more. 44 [48, 52] sts rem.

Knit 4 rnds, or until glove measures about 1.5"/4cm from the thumb hole. If a fitting is possible, have the recipient try on the glove to confirm that this is the correct place to start the little finger, and add or subtract rounds accordingly.

Little finger:
K5 [6, 6], place next 34 [36, 40] sts on waste yarn, use the backward loop method to CO 3 sts, knit last 5 [6, 6] sts of rnd. 13 [15, 15] sts. Work even in St st until finger measures 1.25 [1.5, 1.75]"/3 [4, 4.5]cm, or 0.25"/0.5cm less than desired length.
Next rnd: K1 [0, 0], *k1, k2tog; rep from * to end. 9 [10, 10] sts.

Knit 1 rnd.
Next rnd: K1 [0, 0], *k2tog; rep from * to end. 5 [5, 5] sts.
Cut yarn, thread through rem sts, pull tight and fasten off.

Upper hand:
Transfer 34 [36, 40] held sts to needle. Arrange sts so that beg of rnd is just to the left of little finger. Join yarn leaving a 10"/25cm tail. K34 [36, 40], pick up and knit 3 sts from base of little finger. 37 [39, 43] sts.
Knit 5 rnds.

Third finger:
K5 [5, 6], place next 24 [26, 28] sts on waste yarn, use the backward loop method to CO 3 sts, knit last 8 [8, 9] sts of rnd. 16 [16, 18] sts. Work even in St st until finger measures 2 [2.25, 2.5]"/5 [5.5, 6.5]cm, or 0.25"/0.5cm less than desired length.
Next rnd: K1 [1, 0], *k1, k2tog; rep from * to end. 11 [11, 12] sts.
Knit 1 rnd.
Next rnd: K1 [1, 0], *k2tog; rep from * to end. 6 [6, 6] sts.
Cut yarn, thread through rem sts, pull tight and fasten off.

Middle finger:
Join yarn leaving a 10"/25 cm tail. Knit next 5 [5, 6] sts from waste yarn, pick up and knit 3 sts from base of middle finger. Knit next 5 [5, 6] sts from waste yarn to needle and knit across, pick up and knit 3 sts from base of third finger. 16 [16, 18] sts. Work even in St st until finger measures 2.25 [2.5, 2.75]"/5.5 [6.5, 7]cm, or 0.25"/0.5cm less than desired length.
Next rnd: K1 [1, 0], *k1, k2tog; rep from * to end. 11 [11, 12] sts.
Knit 1 rnd.
Next rnd: K1 [1, 0], *k2tog; rep from * to end. 6 [6, 6] sts.
Cut yarn, thread through rem sts, pull tight and fasten off.

Index finger:
Join yarn leaving a 10"/25cm tail. Knit rem 14 [16, 16] sts from waste yarn, pick up and knit 3 sts from base of middle finger. 17 [19, 19] sts. Work even in St st until finger measures 2 [2.25, 2.5]"/5 [5.5, 6.5]cm, or 0.25"/0.5cm less than desired length.
Next rnd: K2 [1, 1], *k1, k2tog; rep from * to end. 12 [13, 13] sts.
Knit 1 rnd.
Next rnd: K0 [1, 1], *k2tog; rep from * to end. 6 [7, 7] sts.
Cut yarn, thread through rem sts, pull tight and fasten off.

Thumb
Place 14 [16, 18] held thumb sts on needle so that there are 7 [8, 9] sts on each needle tip and rnd begins at outside of thumb (in the center of the 14 [16, 18] sts). Join yarn leaving a 10"/25cm tail.
Rnd 1: K7 [8, 9], pick up and knit 5 sts from CO edge, pm, pick up and knit 5 sts from CO edge, k7 [8, 9]. 24 [26, 28] sts.
Rnd 2: Knit to 3 sts before marker, k2tog, k1, sm, k1, ssk, knit to end. 2 sts dec'd.

48

Rnd 3: Knit.
Rnd 4: Rep Rnd 2.
Rnds 5-7: Knit.
Rnd 8: Rep Rnd 2. 18 [20, 22] sts.
Rnds 9-11: Knit.
Rnd 12: K8 [9, 10], k2tog, knit to end. 17 [19, 21] sts.
Work even in St st until thumb measures 1.25 [1.5, 1.75]"/3 [4, 4.5] cm, or 0.25"/0.5cm less than desired length.
Next rnd: K2 [1, 0], *k1, k2tog; rep from * to end. 12 [13, 14] sts.
Knit 1 rnd.
Next rnd: K0 [1, 0], *k2tog; rep from * to end. 6 [7, 7] sts.
Cut yarn, thread through rem sts, pull tight and fasten off.

Cuff hem:
Turn hem to WS at picot rnd. Unzip provisional CO one st at a time. Using yarn needle and yarn tail from CO, whip stitch each live loop of the CO to the WS of the glove.

LEFT GLOVE
Picot Cuff:
Work as for right glove.
Arrange sts so you have 28 [31, 34] sts for palm on first needle tip, and 30 [33, 36] sts for back of hand on second needle tip.

Wrist and lower hand:
Work charted patterns as follows:
Palm: K5 [6, 8], pm, work Left Palm chart, pm, k5 [7, 8].
Back of hand: K6 [7, 9], pm, work Left Back chart, pm, k6 [8, 9].

When all 45 rnds of charts are complete, 56 [62, 68] sts remain and each needle tip holds 28 [31, 34] sts.
Work middle of hand and thumb hole, fingers, thumb, and cuff hem as for Right Glove.

FINISHING
Weave in ends. Use yarn tails to duplicate stitch over any gaps at base of fingers. Block.

ABOUT THE DESIGNER
Sharon Fuller works as a database developer and enjoys designing knitting patterns as another sort of programming. She brings a dressmaker's eye for detail and a love of surface decoration to her designs. Visit sharonf on Ravelry or blog.sharonmattnadia.com to see more of her design work.

LEGEND FOR ALL EMPYREAN CHARTS
(charts appear on next two pages)

☐ knit

● purl

╲ k2tog

▨ no stitch

⊤ Right Lifted Inc: Use the right needle to pick up the back of the st below the next st on the left needle. Place it on the left needle, then knit into it.

◆ Place bead: Pick up bead with crochet hook and take the st off the needle with the hook (hook will have bead above st on hook). Pull the st through the bead. Place st on right needle.
If omitting beads, simply purl this stitch.

⋋⋌ Left Twist: Knit second st on left needle tbl, then knit first st.

⋌⋋ Right Twist: Bring right needle in front of work and knit second st on left needle, then knit first st on left needle.

⋋|⋌ Left Twist Dec: Knit third st on left needle tbl, do not drop original st from needle. Sl first st from left needle to right needle kwise. Knit next st, drop it from left needle along with the first knit st. Pass the slipped st over. 1 st dec'd.

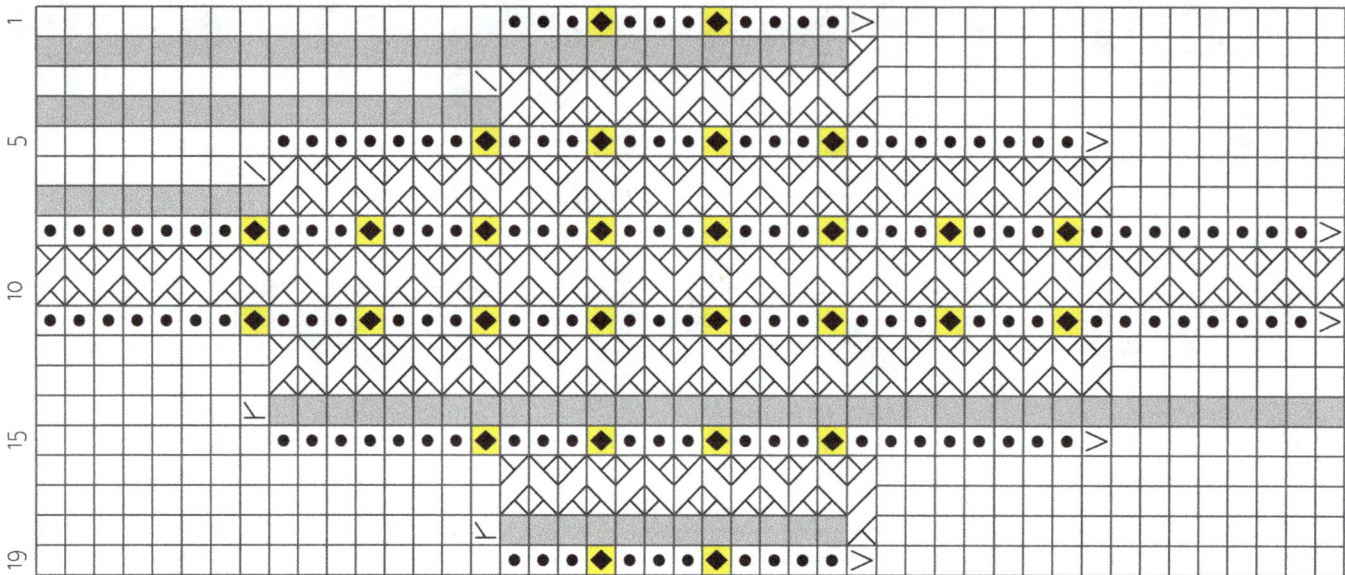

RIGHT PALM CHART ↓

RIGHT BACK CHART ↑

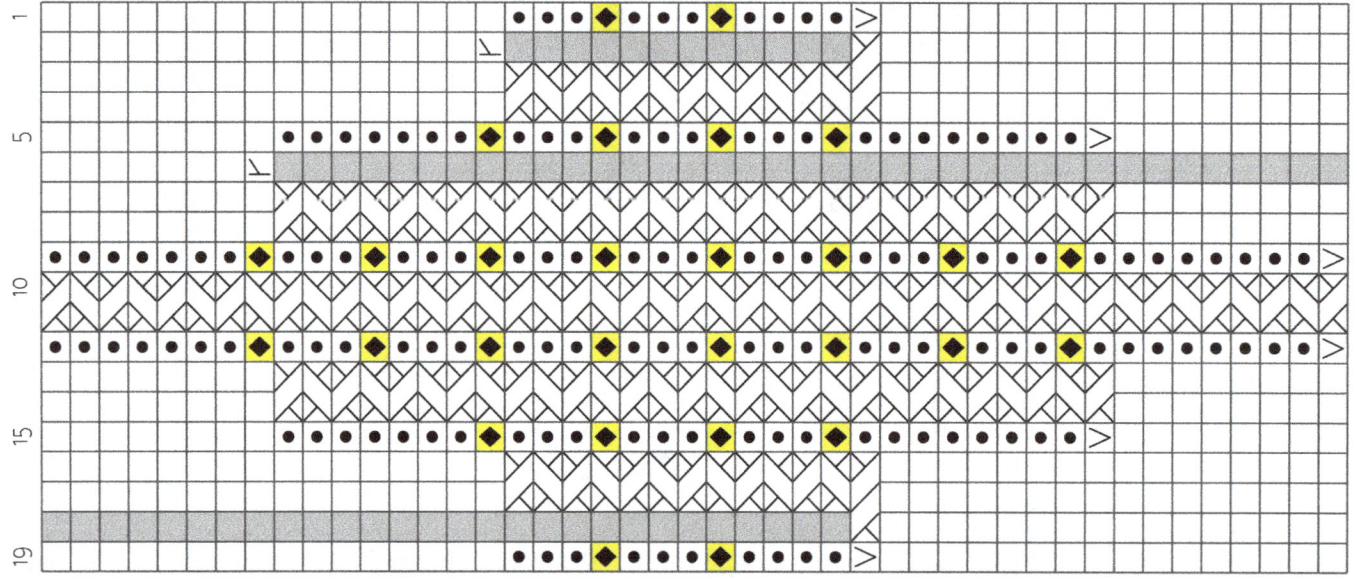

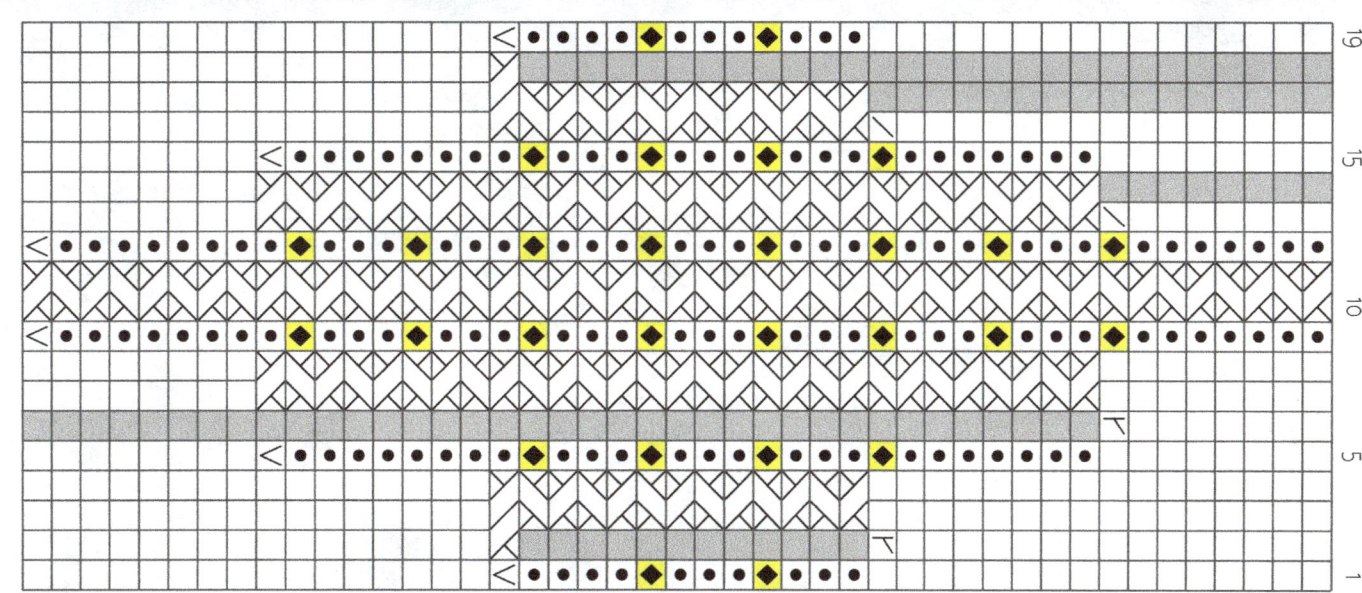

LEFT BACK CHART

LEFT PALM CHART

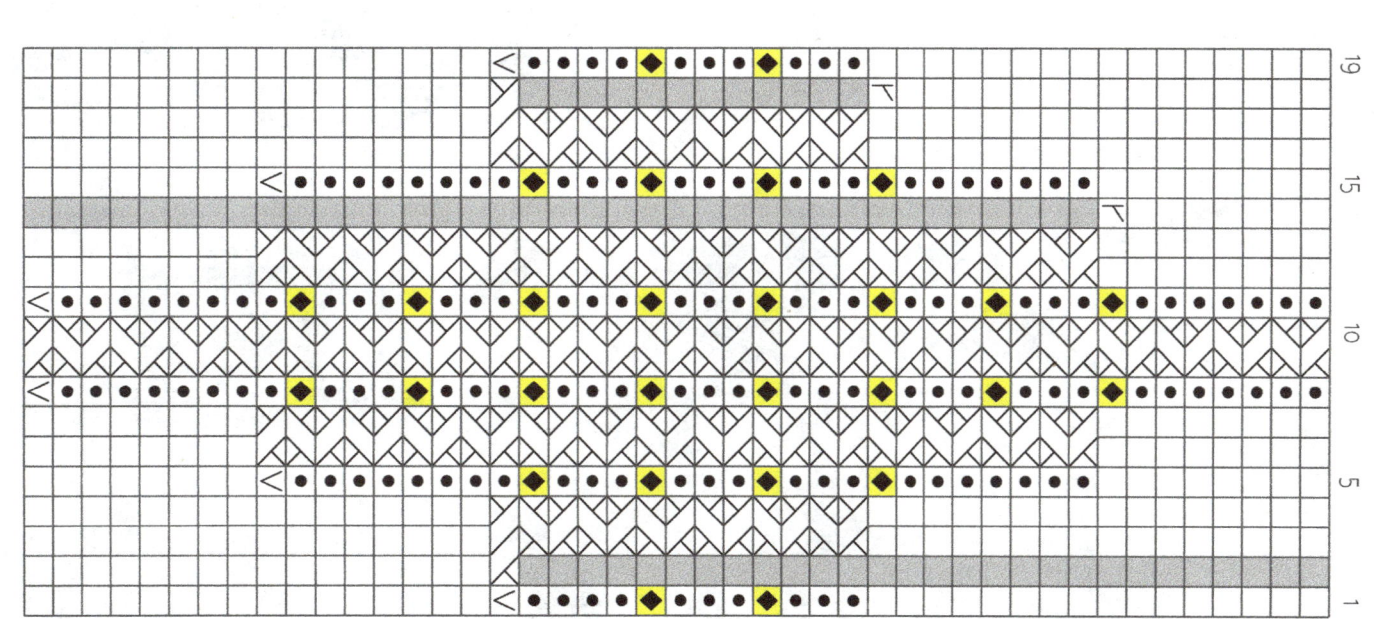

ACKNOWLEDGMENTS

Thank you to the designers who created such beautiful work for the book. Our biggest thanks to photographer Robert Gladys, makeup artist Elle Gemma, and to our models Arabella Proffer, Rachel Harner, Susan Prahst, Shametra Rozzel and Terra Incognita, as well as to Abra Forman, whose considerable talents helped bring the project together in its early stages. Sarah Jo Burch helped keep things running so Abra and Shannon could get things done, and MJ Kim did a massive amount of organizational work before we handed everything off to the talented technical editor, Alexandra Virgiel. Elizabeth Green Musselman came late to the team but helped enormously with wrapping up loose ends.

The book wouldn't be nearly as beautiful without the yarns contributed by the companies below.

We'd also like to thank the generous patrons whose Kickstarter support helped make this book series possible.

YARNS FEATURED IN THIS BOOK:

Cephalopod Yarns (http://cephalopodyarns.com/)
Dragonfly Fibers (http://www.dragonflyfibers.com/)
Indigodragonfly (http://indigodragonflywordpress.com/)
Lisa Souza (http://www.lisaknit.com/)
Needle Food (Unfortunately, Needle Food is no longer in business.)
Schaefer Yarn (http://www.schaeferyarn.com/)
Squoosh Fiberarts (http://www.squooshfiberarts.com/)
Yarn Love (http://www.shopyarnlove.com)

ABBREVIATIONS

approx	approximately
beg	begin/beginning
BO	bind off
CC	contrasting color
cn	cable needle
CO	cast on
dec	decrease(s)/decreasing
dpn(s)	double-pointed needles
foll	follows/following
inc	increase(s)/increasing
k	knit
k2tog	knit 2 together
kfb	knit into front and back of the same stitch
kwise	knitwise
LLI	left-leaning lifted increase
m	marker
m1	make 1 stitch
m1L	make 1 stitch, left-leaning
m1p	make 1 purl
m1R	make 1 stitch, right-leaning
MC	main color
p	purl
p2tog	purl 2 together
patt	pattern
pfb	purl into front and back of the same stitch
pm	place marker
psso	pass slipped st over
p2sso	pass 2 slipped sts over
pwise	purlwise
rem	remain/remaining
rep(s)	repeat(s)
RLI	right-leaning lifted increase
rnd(s)	round(s)
RS	right side
sl	slip
sm	slip marker
ssk	slip, slip, knit these 2 sts together
st(s)	stitch(es)
St st	stockinette (stocking) stitch
tbl	through the back loop
WS	wrong side
wyib	with yarn in back
wyif	with yarn in front
yo	yarn over

ABOUT COOPERATIVE PRESS

partners in publishing

Cooperative Press (formerly anezka media) was founded in 2007 by Shannon Okey, a voracious reader as well as writer and editor, who had been doing freelance acquisitions work, introducing authors with projects she believed in to editors at various publishers.

Although working with traditional publishers can be very rewarding, there are some books that fly under their radar. They're too avant-garde, or the marketing department doesn't know how to sell them, or they don't think they'll sell 50,000 copies in a year. 5,000 or 50,000. Does the book matter to that 5,000? Then it should be published.

In 2009, Cooperative Press changed its named to reflect the relationships we have developed with authors working on books. We work together to put out the best quality books we can, and share in the proceeds accordingly.

Thank you for supporting independent publishers and authors.

We're on Ravelry as CooperativePress. Please join our low-volume mailing list and check out our other books at...

WWW.COOPERATIVEPRESS.COM

ABOUT FRESH DESIGNS

Shannon Okey wanted to do something to showcase emerging design talent after she left the editorship of a UK print knitting magazine; Fresh Designs is the result. A partnership between talented designers and primarily small/indie yarn companies (all of whom are thanked on the previous page — please help support these remarkable companies when you next shop fo' yarn), the first 10 Fresh Designs books have also broken the mold for designer compensation. Each time you purchase a Fresh Designs book or pattern, the designers receive a royalty share.

We hope you'll enjoy meeting the designers in these pages, and that you'll check out the other books in the Fresh Designs series.

55

www.ingramcontent.com/pod-product-compliance
Lightning Source LLC
Chambersburg PA
CBHW081917180426
43199CB00036B/2821